DAVID G. RETTIG

UNF*CK LEADERSHIP!

How to Become a Great Leader in the Midst of Mediocrity.

ISBN 9781697321555

Dedication

This book is dedicated to my wife, Missy, and my mentor, Greg Schuth.

Missy, whenever I come up with some harebrained idea, you say, "I trust you." Thank you for trusting me and loving me, often when I deserved neither. Love you, Babe.

Greg, whenever I think of the best leader I've ever known, I think of you. Period. You encouraged a self-important geek without a college degree and your belief in me transformed me into the leader I am. I am forever in your debt.

I'd also like to thank my children: Rebecca, Charlie, and Benjamin. Being your dad is the best thing that I've ever done. If I never did one other thing with my life, I would feel like it was all worthwhile because of you.

Rebecca, thank you for wanting to be a writer. If you hadn't shared your dream of writing, we would have never started attending the Broad Ripple Morning Writers Meetup and I would have never learned to assemble my random thoughts into a book. I can't wait to see your name on a book cover. Love you, Monkey-Butt.

Charlie, you're ambitious and brilliant. When I was preaching that you should work for yourself, you did it. You showed your dad that a kid with the focus can write computer games and earn a great living while I was still dragging my ass into the office 5 – 6 days a week. You inspired me to go out on my own. Love you, Cheeseburger.

Ben, thanks for embracing your weirdness. I love when you try to make a joke and it falls flat. I love that you know that you can totally be yourself with me and Mom and we will love you no matter what. Stay weird. Love you, Bean.

Never chose to be average.

-- Dad

CONTENTS

PREFACE

"I hate political correctness. I absolutely loathe it." – Simon Cowell

If you read *UNF*CK IT,* you know that my books can piss a few people off. I had to deal with one internet troll who said that I wasn't a serious author because I used the word, "fuck." If you've made it this far, you aren't one of those people.

Generally, people get pissed off before they even read the first page. When writing *UNF*CK IT*, some of my closest friends read the pre-published book. As soon as they saw the title, they said, "Damn, David. Are you sure you want to put your name on *that*?"

My mentor and friend, Greg, once said, "If you ask David for his opinion, you better be ready to hear it."

Hold my beer.

I believe that leadership is fucked, and I want to unfuck it. Which leads me to two important words:

Fucked [/fuhkd/]

Adjective

1. Broken. Not achieving the intended purpose. Failing to function well.
2. In a hopeless situation.

Therefore, when I say, "Leadership is Fucked," I mean: leadership doesn't work, and leadership sometimes feels like a hopeless situation.

And when I say, "Unfuck Leadership", I mean:

Unfuck [/uhn-fuhk/]

Verb

1. Fix. Achieve the intended purpose. Function well.
2. Give hope.

Do you want to unfuck leadership? Me too.

ABOUT THIS BOOK

"Some habits of ineffectiveness are rooted in our social conditioning toward quick-fix, short-term thinking." – Stephen Covey

A quick search on Amazon produced over 40,000 leadership titles with quick-fix solutions. Five easy steps to... The secret of... Leadership Lessons from your-favorite-leader-du-jour. Bookshelves are full books that promise silver bullet solutions. **Silver bullet solutions offer a simple fix to complex problems.** Some common silver bullet solutions are:

- Drink eight glasses of water a day and lose weight!
- An apple a day keeps the doctor away!
- Eat oatmeal to cure heart disease!
- Vote for my favorite politician!
- Chew gum to stop smoking!
- Build a baseball field in your cornfield.
- Set up a website and your business will grow!
- Eat dinners together and your family problems will go away!
- Read these books and you'll be a great leader!
- Listen to this podcast and you'll be a great leader!
- Go to this conference and you'll be a great leader!
- Do this 5-minutes a day you'll be a great leader!
- Throw the ring in the volcano and the evil wizard will die!

Screw silver bullet solutions. Silver bullet solutions do two things really well: sell books and extend the problem. While you're trying the bestselling business-book-du-jour, the problem still exists. But silver bullets are attractive because they are easy and fast. **People like fast and easy solutions**.

As a lifelong fat-ass, I can tell you no fat-ass wants to hear, "I can help you be thin and all it will take is rethinking everything you do, everything you eat, everything you believe about food and exercise, and possibly some of your relationships." I want someone to give me a pill that will make me lose 150 pounds and still let me eat an entire box of Pop-tarts every meal. And don't come at me with that six-pack of Pop-tarts... I want the family-sized twelve pack.

This book isn't another silver bullet solution. This book is a candid, holistic, systems-thinking examination of why leadership is fucked and how to unfuck leadership.

The guidance in this book <u>will</u> unfuck your leadership. But it won't be a quick, easy fix. It will take rethinking everything you do, everything you believe, and possibly some of your relationships.

You should also be aware that **this book contains profanity**. Maybe 'contains' is an understatement. I will often throw in a curse word when it's complete fucking unnecessary. If that offends you, please refer to the title of the fucking book. The book also contains a smattering of sarcasm. For sarcasm, I will use a special font. This one. The one you are reading right now. The same font I use throughout the entire book.

This book is laid out in three major sections. We start with defining leadership and examples of leaders in Section 1: What is a Leader? Section 2: Becoming a Great Leader covers the process of assessing your leadership and creating a process for growing into a great leader. Finally, in Section 3: Leadership Cookbook, I show you some of my favorite leadership tools. You may be tempted to jump to Section 3. It's your book; do what you want, but I wouldn't recommend it. Section 3 refers to concepts in Section 2. Section 2 refers to scenarios in Section 1. You could just ahead, but it's a short book. Suck it up and read it.

WHY DO I CARE WHAT THIS GUY THINKS?

I've leading people for over 12 years. I've led teams with 100+ people at Fortune 500 companies, teams with 3 people at small businesses, and everywhere in between. I've spoken about leadership nationally at groups as large as 1,500. I've coached and mentored leaders and aspiring leaders in the U.S., China, and Africa.

Additionally, I've studied leadership for a long time. I have an MBA, a master's degree in management and leadership, and I'm pursuing a doctorate focusing on leadership. Which means that I've read hundreds and hundreds of some greatest thought-leaders on leadership.

Once in a while, some jackass will come up and say, "You can't study leadership. Leaders are born." They think that because I've studied leadership, they can dismiss my dozen years of actually leading people.

When people hear facts that they don't like, rather than examining their beliefs, they dismiss the facts. One way of dismissing facts is to attack the person presenting the facts. This is called an *ad hominem attack* and it's stupid.

I'll address the origins of leadership in length in a later chapter, but if you believe that leaders are born, I have good news and bad news. The good news is that many intelligent people have shared your opinion. The bad news is that they all died over 300 years ago.

Welcome to the 21st century. We have flushing toilets, electric lights, and social science research about leadership.

Enough foreplay. Let's get to unfucking.

SECTION 1 – WHAT IS A LEADER?

CHAPTER 1: WHAT'S A NICE GIRL LIKE YOU DOING IN A BOOK LIKE THIS?

"We are the books we read..." – Cath Crowley

Hopefully, you are here to learn about being a leader. This means a couple of things: you either are or want to be a leader, and you realize that you don't know everything. That's a great start. Being a leader is important.

Some interesting facts about leaders:

- Most employees are unhappy with their leaders.
- Many employees would willingly give up their raises to screw over their bosses.
- Poor management is the number one reason high-performers leave a company.
- Direct reports of bad leaders have higher heart disease, higher blood pressure, and higher death rates, but lower pay and lower performance.

So you want to be a leader... but do you want to be a <u>great</u> leader?

Economists can teach us a lot about how most people approach leadership. For a long time, economists built economic theories around the assumption that people were logical creatures that made decisions that maximize value and utility. MBA schools taught economic theories based on the behavior of these theoretical rational creatures and MBA graduates spouted these theories as if they came from a burning bush written on stone tablets.

But serious economists doubted this rational behavior. One Nobel laureate, Dr. Richard Thaler put it best when you said, "The purely economic man is indeed close to being a social moron. Economic theory has been much preoccupied with this rational fool."

In response to this rational moron, Dr. Herbert Simon came out with *satisficing*, a *portmanteau* of satisfying and suffice. A portmanteau is smashing two words together to make a whole new word, like spork or clusterfuck. Satisficing is the idea that we look for a solution until things are good enough. we are sufficiently satisfied, <u>not</u> optimizing... satisficing.

Satisficing is how most people approach leadership. They want to a leader and they don't want to be a bad leader. They don't want to *suck*... but as soon as they are sufficiently good enough to not suck, they are done. But good enough is not great.

Becoming great requires effort. A lot of effort.

Becoming a great leader is a little like martial-arts. I'm a black sash in Iron Tiger Kung-Fu. Think Chris Farley in Beverly Hills Ninja. Like that. Only sillier looking. But I can teach you to throw a punch in a second. Hell, you probably don't need my direction for that. Wait...Don't tuck your thumb inside your fist... Jeez... let me show you...

However, teaching you how to throw a punch while feinting a kick and protecting your elbow from hyper-extension, blocking at the same time, drawing power from trapezius muscles, and retracting your fist at the same speed... takes a long-ass time. Oh, and push your tongue to the roof of your mouth. I don't need you to bite your own tongue off if you get uppercut. Don't look at your opponent's eyes. Look at the top of their sternum. I tell you why later. And exhale when you punch. Sometimes people get so caught up in the adrenaline that they forget to breathe. And I need you to do this all without thinking about doing it. It needs to be an instant reaction.

Then when you have all that down, I need your body to harden your bones from years of pounding on something hard. I used to hike with my wife and punch trees to harden my knuckles. If you ever see someone punching trees, you can assume they are martial-artists or hate the Lorax. I punched bags full of dried mung beans until they turned to dust, then soaked my hands in Chinese herbs to heal them.

And that's just the beginning. I only had a first-degree black sash. My instructor at the time held a 9th-degree black sash. That's a lifetime of fighting... and he didn't know it all.

Leadership is the same way. It takes a lifetime to become a great martial artist and it takes a lifetime to become a great leader. And great leaders matter.

Have you ever worked for a bad leader? Remember how they made you feel at work every day? Remember how you felt Sunday night because tomorrow would be Monday and you had to see them again? Remember how you felt after work? You came home drained, exhausted, angry, spent. You didn't have anything left to give your spouse or kids or dog. How did that affect your spouse? Your kids? Your dog?

That bad leader just made your family's life worse and they didn't even know your family.

Have you ever worked for a great leader? Remember how they made you feel? Remember looking forward to doing your job because you knew you mattered and what you did was important? Remember everything you learned from that leader? Remember the amazing things you and your team did? A great leader helps you achieve more than you ever thought you could. A great leader helps you grow and helps you advance and opens new career possibilities.

When you worked with a great leader, you come home energized and excited about your job. You are a better spouse, a better parent, or a better fur-parent because of that great leader, and they didn't even know your family.

Maybe that leader encourages you to return to school. Maybe that leader gives you stretch assignments. Maybe because of that leader you move into a job you love. Maybe you make more money and that education, job, or money enables you to move to a better neighborhood, send your kids to a better school, pay for better medical care for a sick family member, or make a large donation to your favorite charity.

Again, that great leader made a difference in areas they didn't even know about.

People deserve great leaders. Not so-so leaders. **Are you here to be a great leader?**

And to press the martial arts metaphor to the point of breaking, I'll paraphrase Mr. Miyagi, who said, "Walk right side, safe. Walk left side, safe. Walk middle ... sooner or later you get squish like grape. Either you leadership do 'yes', or leadership do 'no'. You leadership do 'guess so' – squish – just like grape."

Plus, you've got people following leaders down this road... squish... We don't need more people walking down the middle of the road. People are following leaders. Get mediocre leaders off the fucking road.

Get off the ducking road...

There is no silver bullet to becoming a great leader. It takes a lifetime of practice. I've been working on it for decades and I've got a long way to go. But this system will get you that black belt in leadership and that's enough to kick ass.

Are you committed to becoming a great leader? Or are you just looking to walk down the middle of the road? Is good enough good enough?

Squish.

Let me tell you one more story about the effect of great leaders.

I was in Orlando, Florida, sitting in a dimly lit restaurant. Mariachi music played in the background. My large round hand-carved wooden table held rows of shot glasses filled with golden, amber, and clear liquids. Surrounding the table sat the CEO of a large company, two of his young sales reps, me, and twenty empty chairs. The twenty empty chairs were supposed to hold twenty asses of twenty other customers of the CEO's company. We were at a business convention, the CEO (Steve), invited a bunch of us to join him for a *cata*, a tequila tasting. Steve was a *catador*, a certified tequila taster, trained to identify over one hundred different characteristics of tequila. He had lined the table with 96 shot glasses, four different tequila shots for each attendee.

As Steve glanced at his Rolex, I asked, "Did the others have a car?" Steve looked at me blankly. I continued, "I only had a car because I was in town on business anyway. Most people don't have a car at these conferences. This place was a haul."

"Well… I guess we get to enjoy this tequila," Steve said. "This is my favorite tequila." He named the brand. Afterward, I found out that CNN covered this premium tequila in 2017 because of the $30,000 price tag.

The cheapest, a silver or plata tequila, was the best thing I had ever tasted. It was smooth leaving a hint of sweet vanilla on the palate. The amber or reposado tasted like the silver tequila had a threesome with

small-batch caramel and Mexican cinnamon and this was the baby. The golden liquid, añejo, tasted like Mexican vanilla and a couple of apples joined the threesome above and turned it into a full-blown gangbang. Like Devito and Schwarzenegger, this baby had a bunch of daddies. The Ultra reminded me of fine bourbon more than tequila, with notes of wood and smoke and burnt sugar. It was the best night that I barely remember, but I kept one of the empty bottles as a souvenir.

You might be asking the point of that story. Here it is: I can't drink cheap tequila now. **Once you've had the good stuff, you can't tolerate the shitty stuff**. It actually offends me when they call that shit "tequila".

I feel the same way about leaders. I am humbled to have worked for some of the best leaders in the world; women and men who modeled what leaders do, how leaders act, how a leader thinks, and how a leader feels. They have invested in me and molded me into the leader I am, not because I am special, but because they are special. And since I've had the good stuff, now I can't stand shitty leaders. They offend me. It's the one thing that instantly pisses me off. One of the leaders in the stories below was such a terrible leader, I took a $20,000 a year pay cut rather than work for them. It was worth $20,000 to me to never see them again. That's how much I hate shitty leaders.

I want you to develop the same intolerance of shitty leaders. <u>You deserve a great leader</u>. Stop. Think about that. YOU deserve a great leader. YOU are worth it. YOU should not put up with some shithead who makes you hate your job. YOU should not let some shithead threaten your life and livelihood because they never learned how to lead people. YOU DESERVE A GREAT LEADER. Say that aloud. Right now. "I deserve a great leader." Say it because it's true. If no one has ever said that to you, I just have.

Now write it down.

Imagine your life if you had a boss who believed in you. A boss who supported you. A boss who wanted you to become the best version of you. What would your life be like?

This book examines real people that I've worked with over my 30+ years of working. All of the names and situations have been changed to protect my own ass. In many situations, some peoples' stories overlapped enough that I mashed the details together to emphasize a point. I draw examples from the stories to illustrate the factors that contribute to successful (and unsuccessful) leaders.

I'm <u>not</u> saying that I'm a perfect leader. By any measure. When people tell me that I'm the best boss they've ever had, it makes me sad for them, because I'm not that good. Kind of like when people tell me that how great the $10 bottle of swill they drink is awesome. I feel sorry for them because there's so much better tequila (and leaders).

But I've learned something from every person that I've worked for. Even if the lesson was only "I never want to be like that jackass."

If you made it this far, I assume that **you want to be a great leader.** I want to develop great leaders. I think we are going to get along great.

And to once again draw on the wisdom of the late great Pat Morita, I will paraphrase Mr. Miyagi again: "We make sacred pact. I promise teach leadership. You promise learn. I say. You do. No questions."

"Never Choose to Be Average."

Rettig Family Motto

CHAPTER 2: ONE WORD ABOUT LEADERS

"Leadership is hard to define and good leadership even harder." - Indra Nooyi

How would you define "a great leader"?

I was sitting in a large cafeteria-style training room of a multibillion-dollar company, under the haze of fluorescent lights, surrounded by this large organization's leaders, from C-level to supervisor. At the front of the room, an overpaid speaker, trained and certified in the leadership stylings of a very famous leadership author, asked the group to "define a leader in one word." After some thought, scores of men and women wrote their definition on 3x5" cards. The speaker gathered the cards and proceeded to write the different definitions on the whiteboard, calling on the authors to explain their definition. In the end, there were thirty unique definitions. The speaker talked about each one, then presented his definition and explained why his definition was the correct one.

Do you see a problem here?

Everyone defined leader differently.

If your spouse sends you to the store to get "milk" and you get tomatoes because to you, "milk" means "tomatoes", you've got a problem. You and your spouse need to share an understanding of the word "milk". Milk needs to mean the same thing to both of you or you are going to have problems.

If you ask two people to define a leader, you will very likely hear two entirely different definitions. If you ask a room full of people in a cafeteria-sized training room, you are likely to get thirty unique definitions (based on a sample study of one). If we can't agree what a leader is, how the fuck can we measure a leader? How do you know if someone is a good leader or a bad leader? How can we hire a leader? How do we do performance reviews on a leader, if we don't know how to measure leadership? How do we know are failing or succeeding as a leader?

But that's only half the problem.

The other problem is suggesting that we **can** define leadership with one word. That's insulting. Tell me everything you love about your spouse... in one word. Tell me about the value of education... in one word. Tell me how to make a cake... in one word. Tell me about a postman or chef or janitor in one word. It's a stupid exercise done by trying-to-be-clever management consultants who offer silver bullet solutions.

> **"Screw silver bullet solutions**. Silver bullet solutions do two things really well: sell books and extend the problem. While you're trying the bestselling business-book-du-jour, the problem still exists."
>
> *Unf*ck Leadership*, p. 3

That exercise minimizes an amazingly complex idea down to one word. If you teach about leadership, never ask people to define something in one word. And If you are in a leadership class and asked to do that, write down, "banana" and if they make you put your name on the card, write the name of the presenter. Because screw them.

DEFINING LEADER

Since this book is about leaders, we are going to be specific about words. It's important that you and I are talking about the same thing. Because if I say "leader" and you hear "tomato", we are going to end up in a weird spot because I have no idea how to unfuck tomatoes.

Some people conflate "leader" and "manager". **When you go to work do you want to be <u>managed</u> or do you want to be <u>led</u>?**

Dr. David V. Day wrote one of my favorite definitions of leaders when he contrasted managerial development, leadership development, and leader development. Day wrote that managers use proven solutions to solve known problems, while leaders learn their way out of unknown problems. That's a complex idea. An example might help.

Imagine that you are a manager. The problem you encounter: one of your team quits and you need to replace them. There is a proven solution (hiring) to a known problem (replacing an employee). You can post the job, set up interviews, select a candidate, and complete the hiring process without having to invent a new solution. That's a manager.

Now imagine that same situation: one of your team quits and you need to replace them, but they had such a rare combination of skills (Think Army Ranger with 10 years of experience as a Brain Surgeon for Unicorns. Yup. You need to find an experienced senior Unicorn Brain Surgeon able to handle themselves during military special operations involving unicorns... not the billion-dollar acquisition unicorns... real magical unicorns). Finding them will be damn near impossible. How will you do that? No one can tell you what to do. You need to figure it out. You need to try things lots of different ideas over and over and hope that one of them "sticks". You need to research other people's solutions to tough hiring problems. Some of your ideas will fail. Hopefully, something will succeed. That's a leader.

I've actually been in situations like that. It sucks because you're trying to figure out what you are going to do and trying ten different things while some unimaginative management wonk tells you to get it done faster or that "you never seem to stick to one thing". If you have one of those, highlight this page and hand them this book.

If someone just handed you this book with this section highlighted, the following paragraph is for you from everyone who is a real leader:

> Rather than bitching about the problem, why don't you try to contribute to the solution? Because you have no fucking idea what to do? Neither do we, but at least we are trying something. So shut the fuck up, go back in your office, and shuffle some papers. Now turn to the person who handed you this book and say, "I'm sorry for being an impotent ass. I will get out of your way", buy a copy of this book, commit to becoming a real leader, and give this book back to the person who gave it to you.

Warren Bennis is often quoted saying, "The manager does things right; the leader does the right thing" which is just a pithy way to say the same thing. A manager ensures that a process is executed correctly ("does things right"). A leader ensures that the organization's processes create the outcomes that the organization needs ("does the right thing"). You need both skills. You need to be able to create new solutions and, when you find something that works, you need to execute those solutions well.

Some people also tend to use "leadership" and "leader" interchangeably. But Dr. Day also did a bang-up job of delineating those two ideas. Leader skills are the interpersonal skills required in formal leader roles, while leadership skills are the interpersonal skills that benefit the overall company's performance. If you do a team-building activity designed to improve communication between the IT department and the finance department, you are doing leadership training. If you hire an executive coach to help a VP improve his public speaking and presentation skills, you are doing leader training.

Prior to this section, I followed the social convention of using "leader" and "leadership" interchangeably but starting now we are going to talk about leaders when we talk about people in a formal role leading people. When I write a leadership, I will be writing about the training and processes that encourage interpersonal development for anyone in the organization. When I talk about managing, I'm specifically talking about the processes that someone in a formal role as a leader needs to ensure the things are done.

That's a ton to remember, so here's some shorthand:

Leader – A person who leads in a formal role.

Leadership – Interpersonal skills used by a leader or others to work better together.

Managing – Executing processes that someone else defined.

CHAPTER 3: A BRIEF HISTORY OF LEADERS

"Most experts and great leaders agree that leaders are made, not born, and that they are made through their own drive for learning and self-improvement." – Dr. Carol Dweck

A long, long time ago, an unusually large caveman beat the shit out of another caveman trying to steal the large rack of brontosaurus ribs off of his foot-powered cave car. His caveman friends saw this and said, "Ugg. Ugg. Ugg ugg. Ugg" (which translates to "Damn, did you see that? Fred just beat the shit out of that other dude. He's so big and powerful. He must be magic. Let's make him head of the Water Buffalo Club.")

I'm not sure that story is completely factual, but that essence of the story is correct. A long time ago, we used to think leaders were born with magic-powers or were touched by God or were selected by the noodly appendages of the Flying Spaghetti Monster. There was something special about leaders. Something mystical. You can't teach being anointed.

Because we believed in anointed leaders, we built the magic people big stone buildings to live in and shiny metal statues and chairs made of swords all melted together. We made the special people royalty and nobles and prophets, and their children and grandchildren inherited their powers because leaders were anointed by God. Not made.

If you weren't a leader, it was because you weren't chosen. Leaders were special because someone <u>chose</u> them.

Then around 450 years ago, a bunch of people got together and said, "Hey, that dude in that big stone building is an asshole. Let's move away." About a hundred years after that those people said, "Hey, that dude isn't any different than the rest of us. Any one of us could live in a big stone building!" Everyone cheered.

After that for about another 150 years we thought that leaders were special types. Not anointed but somehow born! It must be genetics! That's it. Not magic... science!

If you weren't a leader, it was because you weren't born to lead. Leaders were special because they were born that way.

Then about 50 years ago, we started applying scientific theory to leaders. And found out that you can teach leadership. And to paraphrase the cutest animated French rat ever, "Anyone can lead!" But like the angry chef in the same movie, the people in charge stomped their feet and screamed and yelled.

Because if anyone can lead, then leaders aren't special. And dammit... they want to be special.

Some people with formal leader roles still want to believe they are special. Being special makes them immune to criticism. After all the rank and file peasants have no right to critique them!

I believe that <u>the role</u> of a leader is special. The role is special because of the trust people endow in a leader. People entrust a leader to do the right things. Abraham Lincoln put it really well when he said, "Government of the people, by the people, for the people..." To govern means to lead. To paraphrase Lincoln: "Leaders of people, by people, for the benefit of people..."

This is generally the part where some asshole will think, "What about Bob/Fred/Monica/Whoever? They could never be a leader because [insert some judgment about Bob/Fred/Monica]" and then conclude this book is bullshit, I am full of shit, and they can safely dismiss everything that I just wrote, and they can go back to believing they are leaders because they are special.

Let me address the Bob/Fred/Monica example that I certain someone came up with.

Let's say Bob is an asshole. He's rude. He's abrasive. He argues with everyone all the time. If something happened, some earth-shattering, life-changing event bitch-slapped Bob and Bob suddenly <u>wanted</u> to change, do you think it's possible for Bob to change?

Let's say Fred is an introvert. He's so introverted that he can barely speak to another human. If a life-changing event gut-punched Fred and he <u>wanted</u> to change, could he? I'm not saying it's going to be easy or fast. But <u>could</u> he?

Let's say Monica is a terrible boss. She micromanages her employees and belittles them. She dominates others through fear and threats. If she wanted to change...

Of course, you believe people can change. Otherwise, why would you be reading a book about leadership? **You believe people can change because you believe <u>you</u> can change.**

"AH HA!" you may say. "I've got you! What if they don't want to change!! All of your examples require people to want to change. But my boss, Umberto, thinks he's perfect and he doesn't need to change. Therefore... he can never be a leader..."

What if something happened... some earth-shattering, life-changing event happened to Umberto... do you think he could want to change?

Anyone can lead. Maybe they have a bunch of shit to work out, but everyone can lead. If they want to...

And <u>you</u> want to change. <u>You</u> want to be a great leader. You want to apply the lessons in this book... You want to buy copies for everyone you know... you are getting sleepy... get out your credit card... buy more copies... for everyone you know...

CHAPTER 4: THE GOOD, THE BAD, & THE INEFFECTIVE

"Storytelling is the essential human activity. The harder the situation, the more essential it is." – Tim O'Brien

We tell stories because humans are tribal creatures and for millennia, we have learned through stories told around the campfire. Despite the glow of electric lights replacing the campfire, we still learn best through stories. Watercooler talk is story-telling. Recounting your vacation is story-telling. Writing a profanity-filled business book is story-telling.

Workers still gather at their favorite watering hole for cold beverages and commiseration, to share their latest stories of workplace woes. As the empty glasses stack, the work stories get more and more fantastic. Some people call these "war stories".

In grad school, the texts contain tales of stellar successes, fabulous failures, and bumbling blunders of companies. Grad school texts call these "case studies".

My war stories are a few of the leaders with whom I've worked. These stories often represent several people mashed together into a sort of leader-chimera to make a point. I've changed the names and all of the non-essential details (including company descriptions, revenues, and functions) to protect these organizations, the people, and my own ass. The essential points and actions of every story are completely factual and not exaggerated at all. Really.

I worked with Abe. Abe was a bright, ambitious, charismatic new hire. He busted his ass every day, worked overtime, and took on extra responsibilities. Everyone thought Abe was the hardest-working person in the company. When an entry-level manager position opened, Abe saw the opportunity and worked all the harder. He became a little obsessed about getting ahead. In the evenings, he studied policy manuals, test books, and finally got promoted into an entry-level management position! He celebrated with me and a few of his other friends as he moved into this new career.

Abe continued to work-like-a-dog under a senior manager. He studied the senior manager's job, asking for extra responsibilities, working extra hours, and learning everything that he could.

When an opportunity opened at a branch in another city, Abe's boss advocated for Abe. He was the hardest worker she had ever seen. Based on his reputation and stellar reviews, Abe was selected for the position at the remote branch, over two other more experienced people. Abe was on his own, hours from the corporate office.

The team at Abe's branch were all more experienced than he. Two of the people on Abe's team were passed over to allow Abe to be promoted. They smelled Abe's inexperience when he walked in the door, but Abe was cocky and thought his reputation, intelligence, and exceptional work ethic would make him successful here too.

Abe came into the division expecting the same work ethic that he had demonstrated. Within the first month, several of Abe's employees quit, citing his biting criticism of their work. Abe told his team that he could run the entire branch with one-hand tied behind his back and that he didn't need them. The HQ loved Abe's take-charge attitude and his cracking the whip on this underperforming division.

One evening, an employee called in sick when her grandmother died and Abe said, "Your grandmother doesn't work for me. Get your ass in here." The employee quit on the spot.

The now-profitable division couldn't hire fast enough. Between the growth and the turnover, Abe was struggling. The lack of staff and declining morale among the remaining employees caused decreasing customer service scores and reduced operational performance. Abe put in long hours, working seven days a week to keep the branch open.

To cover for the employees fleeing, Abe hired two of his relatives to pick up some of the extra work. This was a violation of corporate policy; however, Abe was the darling of the business and had little accountability being so far from HQ.

Still overworked and understaffed, Abe started cutting corners. And when his staff reported the quality control issues to HQ, Abe explained it as resentment because of his high work standards.

HQ continued to leave Abe unmonitored. Because Abe was working seven-days-a-week, he started cashing personal checks against the petty cash, which was another violation of company policy. Then he started hiding personal expenses as company expenses, justifying it as payment for working 80-90 hours a week, but being salaried at 40 hours.

Fortunately for the company, Abe's personal checks bounced, which finally caught the attention of HQ. The HQ conducted a thorough audit of everything at the branch and noted the severe policy violations. Abe couldn't smooth-talk his way out of the black and white evidence. Abe was fired and only avoided jail by reimbursing the company for all the money he had taken.

War Story: Barely-There-Becki ·

I worked in the same company as Becki, but in a different department. Becki had been with the organization for years. She was never a superstar, but the company loved her loyalty, which they measured in years with the company. Becki was as consistent as clockwork and never made waves. She never pushed for a raise or a promotion and never argued with anyone.

When the current department manager left, Becki fell into the role, mostly due to her consistent performance and loyalty. I'm fairly sure she didn't even apply for the job. She had worked there longer than anyone else in the organization, knew the company processes in her sleep, and could keep the wheels on the bus.

Her department consisted of a small team that supported an essential function in the company. The team was busy, but not overworked; they had exactly the right staffing level to keep things running smoothly.

Becki's team flew under the radar. The job was routine and, as long as everyone did their job, we sort of forgot that Becki's team was there. Her department was in a back corner of the building and things just sort of ran.

Becki's team handled most of the department meetings and customer calls. Sometimes Becki thought that she didn't even need to be there. And so, since Becki's kids were young, she started sliding out a little early to pick them up from school. During her lunch hour, Becki would go to the gym and took a little extra time coming back some days. In the mornings, she would see her kids off to school. Over time, Becki was at her desk less and less but no one, except her staff, noticed that Becki was only working less than 4-hours-a-days.

When she was there, Becki started closing and locking her office door. She explained, "she was on a call." But her staff noticed that there was no light from under the door and occasionally someone would hear gentle snoring coming from her office.

Then Becki started calling in to her team saying she was sick. She would leave a voicemail before her team arrived, complaining of a stomach virus or cramps or a cold at least one day a week. Her team started an office pool, betting on which day Becki would call in. Everyone would pitch in a dollar and when Becki called in, the winners split the pot.

Being a small team, Becki still had individual contributor responsibilities. She had the stuff to do every day to keep things running, but since she wasn't there, her team had to pick up for her slack. The team started resenting how Becki's absences increased their workload. When the company didn't respond to their complaints about Becki, they became demoralized and resentful of Becki <u>and</u> her boss for failing to address their concerns.

The team started taking long lunches and covering for one another. They thought, "Becki's doing it, so we can too." Some of the hourly team started falsifying timesheets as Becki wasn't there to keep them honest. Costs in the department started creeping up and operational performance started to decline.

This went on for over a year until Becki's boss was promoted, and an outsider was hired in the open position.

The outsider saw the condition of the department, listened to the staff, and investigated. The outsider didn't care about Becki's tenure and saw the effect of Becki's absences. Becki and most of the team was fired.

War Story Complaining Clyde

I was consulting in this small business when Clyde joined. The company put me on the interview committee because I had a reputation for telling people the truth, even if they didn't want to hear it. Clyde had worked in large enterprises prior to interviewing at this small business. Furthermore, Clyde was a thought-leader and had written some of the best engineering white papers out there. He wasn't the type of candidate this small business normally saw, but his experience and bona fides were impressive and had the CEO drooling.

After his interview, I brought up concerns about Clyde fitting into a smaller company, but the other managers shut down that conversation by reminding me that they "would be lucky to get someone with so much experience" and that I wasn't an engineer. "Stay in your lane, Rettig."

Clyde knew the small company would be a step-down, but the pay was decent, and the culture seemed a lot more relaxed than the pressure cooker enterprises where he had cut his teeth as the leader of an engineering department. Besides, Clyde thought that his expertise could bring some maturity to this small company.

When Clyde came into the department, he was appalled by everything. The engineers didn't have adequate tools or training, the technology was out of date, the processes were inefficient, and the engineering department had virtually no budget. He couldn't believe what he had walked into. He vacillated between quitting or firing the entire team and replacing everything.

Clyde decided to tough it out and reform the team into the large enterprise team that he wanted to lead. He decided to get the right tools in place first, see who could ramp up to speed, fire the non-performers, and show the company what a real engineering team looked like.

Clyde asked to double his budget, but the CFO said the budgets were locked until the end of the fiscal year. Clyde would need to work with what he had for the next 6-months.

For the first month, Clyde went to every department manager meeting and railed against the abysmal conditions. He used every opportunity with his boss to ask for more money, more resources, and to contrast the efficient, high-tech departments he used to lead to the "cavemen with finger-paints that worked here".

When he couldn't get the tools he wants, Clyde told his boss that his entire team was incompetent and that without a new team, he couldn't help it if the entire engineering department went to hell.

Clyde's team sense Clyde's disappointment. They knew their tools were out-of-date, but they had always made the situation work by working together, keeping their heads down, and only focusing on the essentials. Secretly, the team hoped Clyde would get some resources to make their jobs easier, but also resented his lack of understanding and appreciation of the amazing work they were doing with the tools they had.

After three months of nothing but complaining, the organization realized their hiring mistake and offered Clyde a large severance packaged to resign. The mistake cost the company nearly five times Clyde's annual salary.

WAR STORY: DOUG DEALS WITH THE DEMORALIZED

I worked with Doug at this company. Doug came into a bad situation. The former head of IT had demoralized the team to the point where there was no organizational trust. The team was outwardly hostile to leaders and didn't need another manager to come in, make unrealistic demands, and force them to work 60-hours a week.

Furthermore, Doug was a business person, not an IT person. He didn't have the technical acumen to vet the needs of the IT team. If they pulled the wool over his eyes, Doug would need to rely on his instincts to approve or deny purchases, and Doug knew that instinctual decisions were a shitty way to run a business.

Doug started by meeting each team member one-on-one. During the introduction, one of the senior IT staff screamed at him, "You don't know what the fuck you are doing, do you? We don't need another pencil pusher. We need some help." Doug tried to reassure the staff that he *was* there to help. The individual meetings confirmed his worst fears. He found a team on the brink of imploding, leaving the organization which needed the IT team in a bad spot.

Doug asked each of the team members two questions, "What should we do more of?" and "What should we stop doing?" He listened and took copious notes. He only asked questions to clarify and understand the problems. At the end of each meeting, he said, "I trust you" and "I'm here to help you."

After the meetings, Doug analyzed his notes. The team was overworked, under-resourced, under-trained, under-appreciated, and in a technological environment crumbling under the weight of complexity and age. In addition, many members of the team complained about a senior person on the team named Joe. Doug knew he had to act fast.

During his first two weeks, Doug had learned that Joe coached his daughter's little league team. Doug talked to Joe about how the team viewed him and drew an analogy to Joe's coaching. Doug said the team needed Joe's experience, but his critical attitude was hurting his relationships with the team. Doug said, "I can help you turn this around. It will be a lot of work, but I'm willing to do it if you are. If you aren't willing to do the work, just let me know." Joe quit the next week. After Joe left, several members of the team thanked Doug for getting rid of him, but Doug saw it as a personal failure.

Doug used the "honeymoon" period of his new position to get some extra budget for the team and spent that money on training his team to demonstrate that he cared about them. He needed to overcome the team's belief that they were only there to do a job. They were an important part of the organization.

These two early-wins demonstrated to the team that Doug had listened and was committed to making the hard decisions and fixing things, but it still took a long time for the team to re-establish trust in the organization and the leaders, but by consistently advocating for the team, Doug turned the team into a high-performing contributor to the organization.

War Story: Emailing Elle

Elle's now a good friend of mine. I may have come into this story late, but I know all the parties involved. Elle was a VP in a Fortune 500 company. Her team consisted of over 5,000 people in an organization spanning the globe. A 70+ hour work week was typical, but Elle was driven and hard working.

In addition to her leader responsibilities, Elle was the face of her company's product for one market. She spoke at least monthly to groups containing hundreds of customers. During these presentations, she would be on stage for four to eight hours a day talking and then would shake hands and take selfies with customers who wanted to post a picture of themselves with Elle. After all, a picture with Elle looks great on your social media feed.

After a long day, Elle just wanted to go to her hotel room and call her kids, but she knew the office email was piling up. As she cleared out the emails, one email appeared from Ian, a staff-level worker at a very small customer of Elle's company. Ian was considering getting an MBA and asked Elle for advice. Elle replied to the email, offering to talk with Ian the following week.

A week later, the appointment reminder popped-up, Elle set aside the fifteen other urgent issues, called Ian, listened to his situation, and gave her best counsel. Ian reminded her of herself a little. She had returned to graduate school later in life to better herself. In addition, she saw a spark in Ian – something that would make Ian a great leader, if he had the right mentor. She said, "Let's talk again in a month." Ian gratefully accepted.

The monthly meetings became a regular event. Elle loved seeing the growth in Ian. Ian was humbled and shocked that Elle would take time away from her sizable team to talk to him. Elle encouraged Ian and offered her experience and advice to guide Ian, and Ian gobbled up the advice, as he admired Elle.

Eventually, his company noticed the same spark in Ian that Elle had noticed and gave Ian a small team. Ian worked hard to invest in each of them, just like Elle had invested in him. He looked for something special in each of them, something that he could grow, and he loved them like he loved his own kids. When his team grew, Ian felt a little like a proud father, although he never said that aloud.

When Elle's business colleague mentioned he was looking for a new IT supervisor, Elle recommended Ian. Ian knew he would be leaving a company where he had a lot of credibility and would be starting over, but trusted Elle's recommendation. Ian worked his ass off, modeled his leadership after the care that Elle had demonstrated to him. The new company recognized something special about Ian's leadership and he got promoted to leading a larger team. Then very large teams. He always felt indebted to Elle for investing in him and committed himself to invest in others.

Ten years later, the customer met Elle at another conference and thanked her. Elle's advice had changed his life and his career. Ian was in a job that he loved because of Elle's advice. And now he led a team with a multimillion-dollar budget and had remained a loyal customer because of his relationship with Elle.

War Story: Fix-it-Fred

I worked for Fred when he accepted an executive position at a family-owned company in desperate need of a turnaround. Poor financial decisions, under-investment in the infrastructure, and declining quality and productivity had created an organization bleeding money. Without significant changes, they had less than five years until the doors closed. Hundreds of people depended on this company for a job and Fred sensed the weight of the project. It was a big job, but Fred felt like he was up to the challenge; he had a reputation for turning around poor performing organizations and had done so in the past.

After a year, through strategic management and process improvement, Fred took the company from losing millions of dollars a year to a marginally profitable organization. The President of the company, Taylor, publicly and privately praised Fred for saving the company and hundreds of jobs.

But Fred saw even more potential. To take them to the next level, Fred knew significant changes needed to happen throughout the company. Fred looked for more areas where he could improve the company.

Taylor, the President of the company, didn't offer any guidance to Fred on this new focus. The most that Fred could get from Taylor was periodic rants about how he wasn't happy with the performance of this department or that project. But no specific direction or goals.

When Fred attempted to assist in the low-performing areas, he often faced resistance. The President of the company had set up the problematic processes and didn't want to change them. If the President had hired a poor performing employee, he would let Fred fire them. In one case, the brother-in-law of the President cost the company half-million-dollar sale, but Fred's hands were tied.

Furthermore, the President would often criticize Fred's thwarted attempts to help. Fred would attempt to fix something, Taylor would resist the change, and a month later bring it up as "another harebrained idea of Fred's."

Eventually, Fred became frustrated by the President's impotent rants, failure to act, and lack of guidance. Fred put together his comprehensive analysis of the company, his recommendations to fix it (including the changes Taylor had thwarted), and how much it would save the company. The plan looked at every department, every employee, and every process to address the President's complaints.

Fred socialized the plan internally and the other department heads loved it. He felt confident that he was on the right track.

When Fred presented his broad-sweeping plan to the patriarch of the company, it fell flat. Fred didn't understand why Taylor was resisting, thinking his success over the last year and the support of the other departments would have demonstrated that his recommendations were credible, actionable, and correct.

Fred knew that the President disliked weak personalities, so he pushed back. He insisted that the organization make the changes to reach their full potential. Red-faced, the President pulled Fred out of the meeting. He told Fred that he was overstepping and should narrow his focus to his area. Fred pushed back again, not understanding why the President wouldn't want him to help the entire company the way he had helped his area.

A month later, the President told Fred that he was no longer needed and immediately ended Fred's role. Fred left, completely lost as to why things had gone south so fast.

War Story: Grace's Games

I was actually one of the three managers in this story. I chose to use the names Thomas, Richard, and Harold to disguise the other participants.

Thomas, Richard, and Harold were department managers who applied for a Director position in their company. All three were more than capable of doing the job. The company interviewed them along with an external candidate named Grace.

Grace exuded executive presence. She was beautiful, athletic, bright, and charismatic. She had polished her resume to the nth-degree and knew all of the right things to say during the interview for Director. Her resume had some job-hopping, but Grace explained that away, telling tales of promised promotions denied, outgrowing her employers, and exceptional opportunities.

Grace dazzled the interview team and got the job. Thomas, Richard, and Harold were shocked that all three of them were denied. They would now report to Grace.

During the first month, something seemed wrong to the three department managers. They had worked together with the former Director and had met as a group, but Grace didn't want that. She wanted individual meetings with each department. During the one-on-one meetings, Grace told each department manager that the others had been bad-mouthing them and had been jockeying for position with Grace.

But Grace didn't know that Thomas, Richard, and Harold were friends and often hung out after work to compare notes. They sensed that she was pitting them against each other, and they agreed to have no part in Grace's games.

Grace started micromanaging the three departments, asking to be CC'ed on all emails between the department managers. When the department managers collectively refused, Grace told her boss that the managers were attempting to undermine her.

Thomas, Richard, and Harold generated reports for Grace from a computer system that was ticking along and able to meet organizational objectives. Grace hated it. Rather than learn, Grace made the case with the executive team that the company needed to change the reporting software: a multiyear, multimillion-dollar investment. She told tales of easy-to-use software and sewed unfounded fears that the current solution would not grow with the company. Her charismatic presentation convinced the company to invest five years and over $10 million dollars to change the software.

One of the department managers, Harold, knew Grace's old boss and took her out to lunch. When Harold said, "I work for Grace now", Grace's former boss said, "Good luck. She's a piece of work" and shared a tale of political maneuvering and backstabbing that led to Grace's entire team quitting at his company. Grace's old boss said, "If she hadn't left, we were planning on firing her."

When the other managers heard this story, they collectively went to Grace's current boss and shared the tale. Grace's boss dismissed the stories as sour grapes from the three being denied the promotion.

Grace's boss told her about the complains and Grace decided to fire Harold, as the instigator. She asked Harold's second-in-command, Ann, "Would you be interested in Harold's job?" The second that the meeting was over, Ann called Harold and told him about the entire meeting.

Harold met with Grace the next morning with a recording device in his pocket. He said, "Ann called yesterday and said you offered her my job." Grace stammered and denied everything. Harold said, "I've worked with Ann for six-years. I hired Ann. Ann is incapable of lying." Grace said that Ann probably misunderstood and that she wasn't saying Ann was lying. Harold said, "If you want to fire me, why don't you act like a leader and just do it instead of being a little weasel" and stormed out of the office.

Harold played the recording for Ann, then called a recruiter and found another job the same day. He returned to Grace's office with Ann and quit. Then Ann quit as well.

Thomas and Richard quit over the next year.

When the managers quit, Grace's games started affecting the remaining staff. Harold's entire team quit two months after he and Ann had. Another team was gone six months later. The last team dissolved after a year. Grace, once director of three departments, was left with a single employee. Her reputation among the tight-knit technical community was so bad that no one wanted to work for her.

She left the company to accept the CIO position of yet-another-company that believed Grace's tales of promised promotions denied, outgrowing the company, and exceptional opportunities.

WAR STORY: MAKING A LIST, CHECKING IT TWICE

And lastly, I worked for Hans. Hans led our team of about twenty IT professionals, some programmers, some network engineers, and some systems administrators. Every Monday, Hans called the entire team together in a large meeting room with a large conference table. Hans pulled out a clean tablet of yellow paper and motioned to his right. The developer to Hans' right recounted everything they did, every meeting they attended, and every person with whom they talked the previous week, while Hans scribbled copious notes on his yellow pad. If the report took less than 10 minutes, Hans would look up from his pad and, with his voice dripping with disappointment, say, "That's it?" If the report was satisfactory, Hans would say, "What's on your plate this week?" and continue his scribbling while the developer recited his tasks for the upcoming week. Some of the kiss-asses liked to talk for thirty or forty minutes, but the average was twenty minutes. Multiply that by twenty people and you find we spent six and a half hours with no lunch break listening to a droning recitation that would have made a boring email. I would do <u>anything</u> to avoid these bureaucratic Bataan death marches. I would schedule work for 10 PM Sunday night, work from 10 PM – 6 AM Monday, and leave before Hans got in, just to avoid the meeting.

Hans felt like the Monday meetings helped him "stay on top of things" and if he didn't hold the team accountable, they wouldn't do anything. Hans also used the long list of activities to justify his department's existence. If they were doing a lot of things, they must be valuable.

When Hans retired, we found a Brazilian-rainforest-worth of yellow notepads stored in rows of file cabinets.

WAR STORY: YOUR STORY

Now I want you to take a few minutes and write down your story. Think of a leader. It could be the best boss you ever had, the worst boss you ever had, or a leader who didn't matter and didn't make one bit of difference in your job. Write down a few details, just so you can learn from your experience. Do this before you move forward, because you are going to come back to see if the systems-thinking analysis that follows, makes sense in your situation.

_____

_____

_____

_____

_____

_____

_____

_____

CHAPTER 5: WHAT WOULD YOU SAY YOU DO HERE?

"You can control two things: your work ethic and your attitude about anything." – Ali Krieger

We just read the true stories about people who ranged from inspirationally brilliant leaders to people who literally destroyed the careers of the people who worked for them. The variability of the quality of leaders is part of the problem. People don't come with warning labels: "Ineffective Leader: May Cause Low Productivity, Decreased Morale, and High Employee Turnover." Wouldn't it be awesome if they did?

Leaders are people and people are complex. You can't define a person in one word and it's useless to try the same thing with leaders. But we can put a definition around leaders.

Leaders are a sum of aptitudes, attitudes, abilities, and actions.

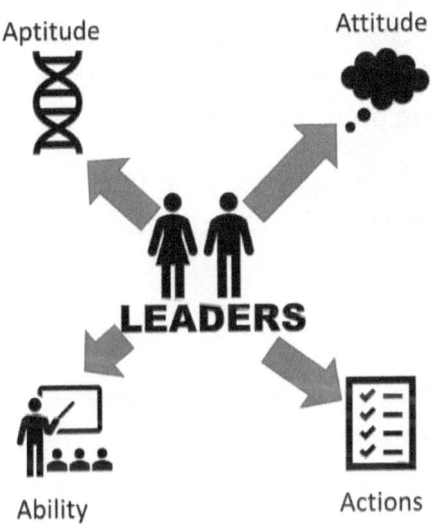

ATTITUDES

Attitudes are the beliefs a leader holds about themselves and others. Attitudes are generally emotional, not rational.

A leader's attitude answers questions like:

- Are people generally honest or dishonest?
- Do people generally work hard or slack off?
- Are people trustworthy?
- Are you better than other people?
- Are people naturally more skilled at some things than other things?
- Is intelligence fixed?
- Do businesses have a social responsibility?
- Is training valuable?
- Should a subordinate give negative feedback to their boss?
- Are different races or genders better suited for different jobs?

Because attitudes are emotional, some of the questions provoke emotions. You might have read a question and thought, "How dare he ask that?" or "That's not a belief! That's a fact!" or "I hate that people feel that way" or "I'm proud of my beliefs."

Because attitudes are <u>emotional</u>, it's hard to change emotions. In fact, logic and reason almost never work to change emotions.

APTITUDE

Aptitudes are the things that seem to come easier to us without a lot of effort. Some people might call it "genetics", some people might say this is the result of early environment, Freud might say its because of your bowel habits (ick), or some might think its aliens or ghosts or your former life... I'll let other people argue over that. I'm not arguing why...

I'm acknowledging that some things seem easier for some people than others.

For example, when I was young, you couldn't shut me up. My mom has an audio tape of me babbling for over an hour (for the non-gray-haired, a "tape" was a little plastic box filled with a magnetic ribbon that you could record sound on for playback later. Like the record button on your phone). I was four or five and just wouldn't shut up. I don't know how she put up with my shit. Sorry, mom. I had demonstrated an aptitude for rambling.

Another story from when I was little: I couldn't keep a beat. Like snapping or clapping with the music. Not a single beat. I was terrible. I had a kindergartner gym teacher who nearly had a mental breakdown while teaching me to clap with the music. (I'm imagining a few of my friends laughing at this and commenting about how white I am... Fuck you guys ⍰.)

So when I was little, I demonstrated an *aptitude* for talking but no *aptitude* for rhythm.

ABILITY

An ability is an acquired talent, something that you can learn. Examples of abilities are writing profanity-filled business books, competitive eating, horseback riding, fencing (with an epee or stolen goods... no judgment...), public speaking, or chess... all the things you can learn...

Leaders learn all sorts of things. How to coach people, how to hire great people, how to encourage collaboration, how to unfuck leadership...

Abilities can be acquired through formal training, self-education, modeling, mentoring, coaching, or the school of hard knocks. All of these are valid methods of acquiring new leader abilities.

The value of a skill depends on its application. The value of a skill is in the application of that skill. Martial arts can be used for picking fights or to quote Mr. Miyagi, "Rule Number One: Karate for defense only." Are you going to be Daniel-san or be Johnny? Sure, William Zabka is way cooler than Ralph Macchio, but Macchio ended up with Elisabeth Shue. Elisabeth...ahhh... my teenage crush...

ACTIONS

> "To be is to do"—Socrates.
> "To do is to be"—Jean-Paul Sartre.
> "Do-be-do-be-do"—Frank Sinatra.
>
> *A T-shirt that made me laugh.*

Leaders do things. Really. You can't just have a great attitude, aptitude, and ability and not do shit. At least not for long... unless you have tenure or are the boss... or have some really embarrassing pictures of the boss... then you're golden...

Actions are the things you do. Things like "talk to the team", "think about the future strategic direction", or "resolve personnel problems."

APTITUDES

Wait a minute...what about aptitudes? I put aptitudes last because they only matter as much as you allow them to matter.

48

Aptitudes are like the safe-harbor statements at the beginning of financial disclosures. Aptitudes are a part of our leadership, but not a reliable source of predicting leadership.

Safe Harbor

Aptitudes may contribute to predictions, guesses or other forward-looking predispositions. While these forward-looking statements might represent what the future holds, they are subject to attitudes, abilities, and actions that could cause actual results to differ significantly. You are cautioned not to place undue reliance on aptitudes.

David G. Rettig

Remember that aptitudes are things that seem to come easier to people without a lot of effort. This could be the result of genetics, early environment, magic, aliens, or something else. The source of aptitudes isn't important for this discussion.

People learn to overcome their aptitudes. One of the best public speakers I know hates being in front of crowds. He learned to overcome his natural shyness. In high school, our valedictorian didn't have the highest IQ, she just worked her ass off. My kung fu instructor, Grand Master Matt Mollica of Ho-I, used to say that naturally strong, fast people made poor instructors because they never had to learn to overcome their limitations. Yes... my fat ass has a black belt in iron tiger kung fu... proof that you can overcome anything.

Grand Master Matt Mollica of Ho-I presenting a black sash to the human equivalent of the Kung-Fu Panda.

Because people learn to overcome their natural limitations, aptitudes can be harder to assess. **Your aptitudes <u>contribute</u> to who you become, but they don't define who you could become.**

There are no good, bad, or useless aptitudes. Aptitudes are just natural tendencies. It's important to recognize that you have natural tendencies, but your natural tendencies don't need to define you.

My daughter used to say, "I'm shy." (She wasn't). She loved meeting people but felt anxious <u>before</u> she met them. After she met them, she turned into a bubbly, hyper-excited talking machine... but the anxiety beforehand, she called, "shy".

Whenever she said, "I'm shy", I would reply, "How's that working for you?" She'd say, "Not good." I'd say, "Then change."

How do you define yourself? Shy? Critical? Dumb? Smart? Gregarious? Relaxed? How's your definition of you working for you? Are you going to let yourself be defined by that word?

Then change.

WHICH MATTERS MOST?

You might ask which matters more: Aptitude, Attitude, Abilities, or Actions?

Which do you think? Really. Take a minute before you move forward. Which do you think matters the most? Your answer might teach you something about yourself:

I think _____ is the most important.

Before we look at your answer, let me tell you a story:

I was at a large conference with over 50,000 attendees. The speaker did an amazing job. He connected with the audience. He told his story from a poor kid with no prospects to a major organizational leader. I saw tears in some eyes. His story hit my heart. My kids would say, "He gave me the feels."

Was the speaker born with the aptitude? Did he just have a can-do attitude? Did he learn the ability to speak in front of large groups? Did he just do the action? Why was he successful? Can we isolate it?

If you believe he was born with natural speaker talent, it would be easy to say, "He is really talented. I could never do that." If you believe that, you don't need to try. You are born with it or not. It's not your fault. It's genetics or magic or being chosen...

If you think it's just an action, he did it and it just happened to work out, it's easy to say, "He was lucky, or he had a good story. I could never do that."

51

If you think it's an attitude, he believed he was a good speaker and therefore he was, you can say, "I don't need to *do* anything. I just need to *believe,* and it will happen." My dad used to say, "Wish in one hand and shit in the other. See which one fills up first." Let me warn you: it's the hand full of shit. Really.

But if you think that the speaker learned to be a great speaker, you would be right.

One of my friends works with the speaker and after the presentation, I said, "He's amazing. Really talented speaker."

My friend said, "You know what's really amazing? He hates public speaking. He's crazy nervous, every time. He constantly second-guesses himself. But he's learned to do it."

He learned to do it. He learned the ability to speak in front of large crowds.

I'm not dismissing the importance of aptitude, attitude, and actions. In fact, being good at something (aptitude) often leads to investing time in learning it (ability). It also might influence our beliefs. If we have a natural affinity for math, we might believe (attitude) that math is easy and people who struggle with math are stupid or lazy. Aptitude leads to actions. If we have a natural affinity for math, we might do more math. If we do not have a natural affinity for math, we might avoid math. Aptitude influences ability, attitude, and actions.

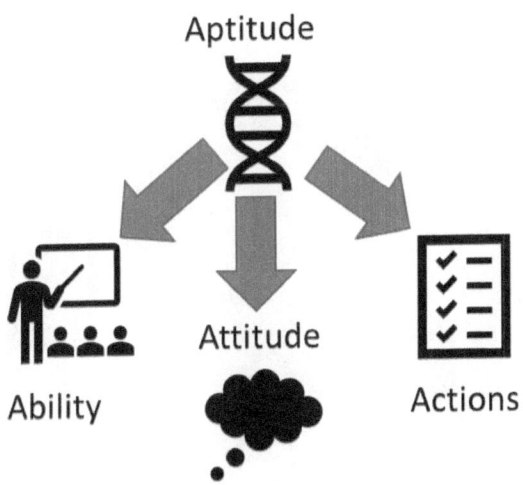

Aptitude

Attitude

Ability

Actions

Furthermore, your attitude about something affects your abilities and actions. If you believe (attitude) that public speaking can't be learned, you will not bother with taking public speaking training. If you believe that leadership is inborn, why would you possibly try to learn it? If you believe that you are bad at public speaking, you will avoid doing it. If you believe (attitude) people aren't trustworthy, you may micromanage (action) them.

But here's something mind-blowing: your attitude affects your aptitude as well. Many cultures believe that IQ is an aptitude; you are born with a fixed-level of intelligence and that's it. In those cultures, IQ varies little. However, some cultures believe that you can improve your IQ. In those cultures, people have increased their IQ by as much as 20 points through study and hard work. Dr. Carol Dweck is a Stanford psychologist and the foremost researcher on the effects of your beliefs on performance. If you want to learn more, I strongly suggest reading her amazing book, *Mindset*.

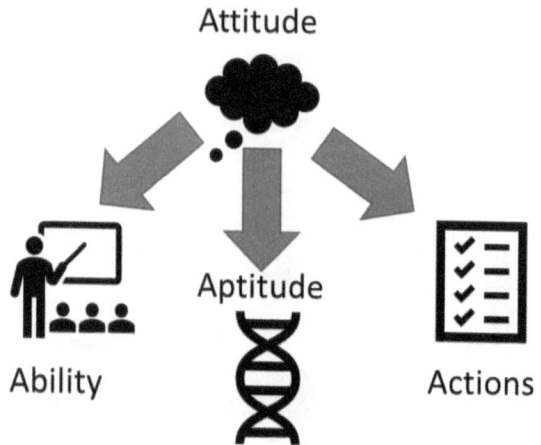

Your training (ability) also affects your actions, attitude, and aptitude. If you believe (attitude) that training affects your IQ, you may decide to pursue training and that learning (ability) could improve your IQ (aptitude).

If you get training (ability) in cooking, you are more likely to perform cooking (action). If you get training in public speaking, you may believe (attitude) that you <u>can</u> speak publicly.

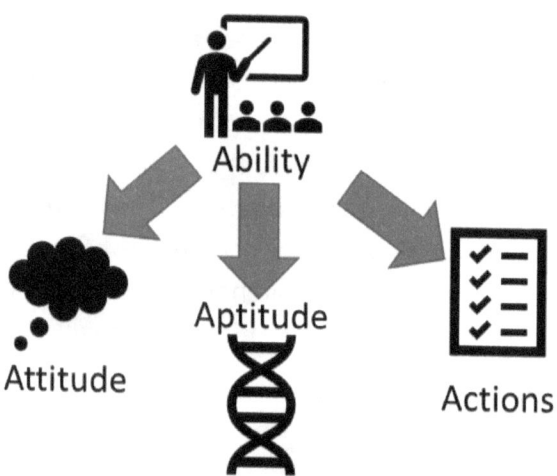

Guess what? Actions affect the other three as well.

As you do something (action), you get better through practice (ability). Research has shown that forcing a smile (action) makes you feel more positive (attitude). Even standing in the Wonder Woman or Superman pose (action) has been shown to increase self-confidence (aptitudes).

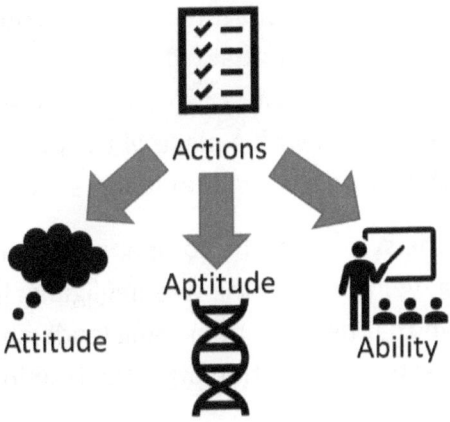

Because of this interdependent system, we end up with an expanded definition of leadership.

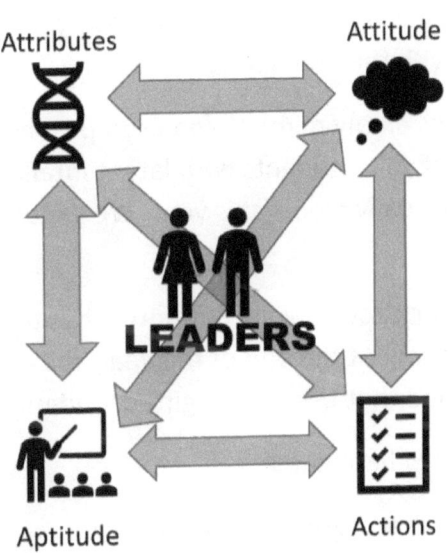

This interdependent system is why most leadership training <u>doesn't work</u>.

Many leadership books deal with attitudes. One cute little leadership book focuses exclusively on attitudes, saying, "Have a positive attitude. Be creative. Trust people." Great attitudes. But if you have a positive attitude and don't demonstrate that with actions, forget it. Another book talks about the characteristics of leaders. Some create great action plans. They each deal with a piece of the puzzle but fail to address the self-reinforcing system that leaders are in.

Failing to address the system is why companies billions of dollars on leadership training, yet the outcome was negligible. In fact, some research has shown that people undergoing leadership training are more likely to leave the organization <u>after</u> the training.

But the interdependent system is even more convoluted.

Imagine a classroom full of elementary students. Bright eyes full of promise. Likely staring blankly into their smartphone. Erase that. Bright eyes – no smartphones. Two researchers enter the classroom and give them a fun little series of challenges. They record the results, analyze them, then meet with the teacher.

"Miss Crump?" (Yes, in my mind, Helen Crump is the teacher) "We've identified several of your students with latent intellectual giftedness. We expect them to really bloom this year. We expect a significant jump in their intelligence."

Miss Crump runs her class as usual but notes that the latent gifted students are blooming. At the end of the year, the researchers retest the students and find that the "latent gifted students" are now gifted.

This research actually happened.

"What the point of that story?", you might ask.

I'm glad that you asked. The "latent gifted" students were chosen completely at random. Yup. It's called the Pygmalion effort or the Rosenthal-Jacobson effect (after the two researchers) and has been duplicated over and over and over... in classrooms and sports <u>and business</u>.

In companies, the Rosenthal-Jacobson effect has shown that if a leader <u>believes</u> an employee is trustworthy, the employee is less likely to steal. If a leader <u>believes</u> an employee is a superior performer, they are more likely to be a superior performer. If a leader <u>believes</u> an employee is a slacker, the employee is more likely to underperform. If a leader <u>believes</u> an employee is a thief, they are more likely to steal.

A leader's attitude influences their subordinates' performance. Thus, the diagram expands.

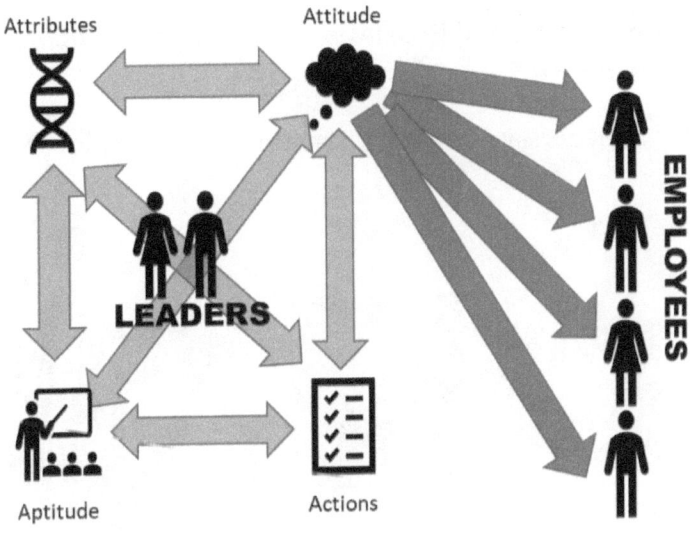

We also know that the actions of leaders affect the engagement of their employees.

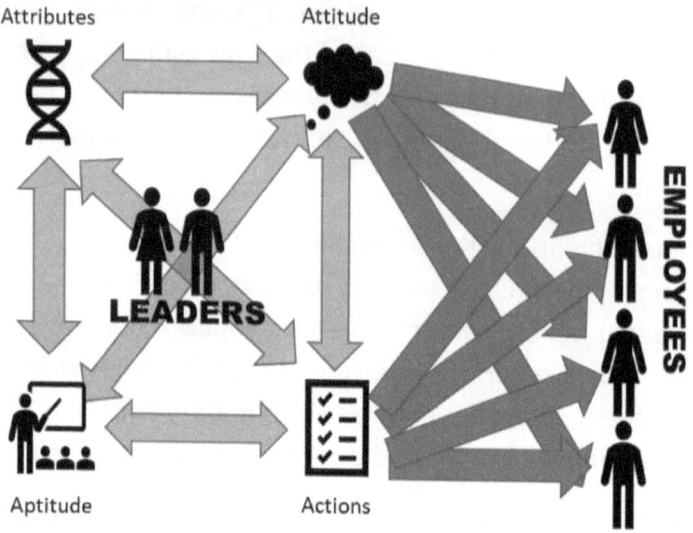

Each leader also is affected (to a lesser extent) by their subordinates' attitude toward them.

Furthermore, leaders are generally someone else's employee.

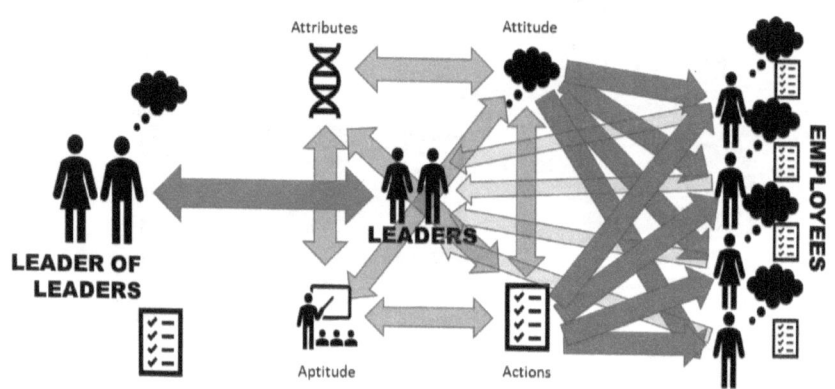

This spider web of self-reinforcing aptitudes, attitudes, actions, and abilities defines the culture of an organization. Sociologists define culture as the beliefs, behaviors, and characteristics common to the members of a particular group or society. We can see how the collective attitudes, abilities, aptitudes, and actions of the people of an organization create a culture and **that culture becomes self-reinforcing.**

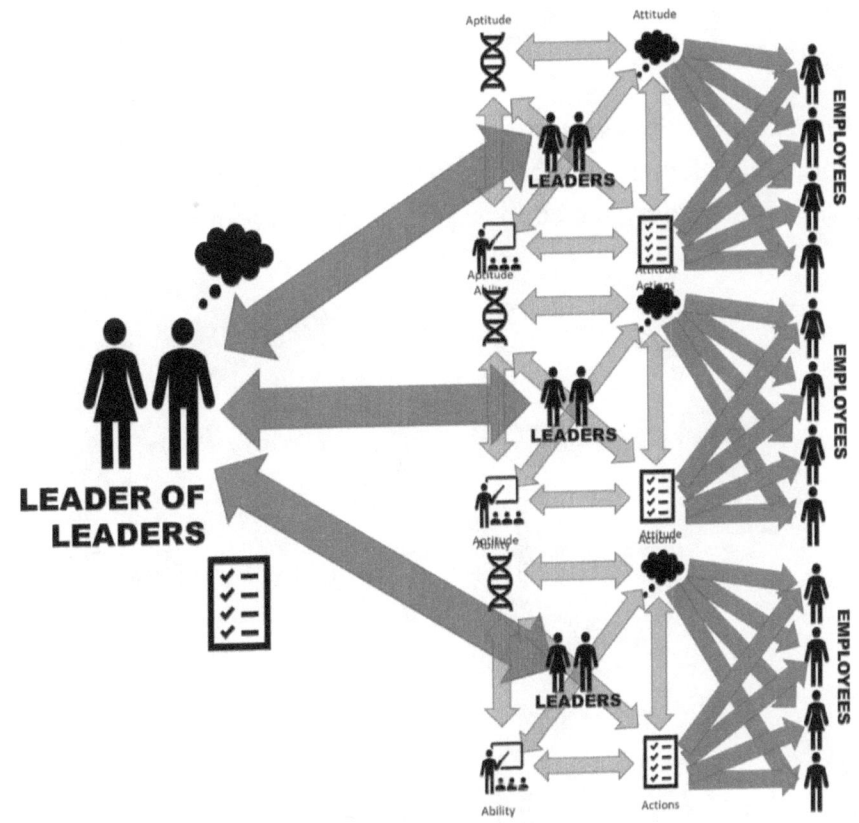

The self-reinforcing nature of organizational culture is why unfucking leadership is <u>incredibly difficult</u>. If you try to change the organizational culture by introducing a new element into the organization...

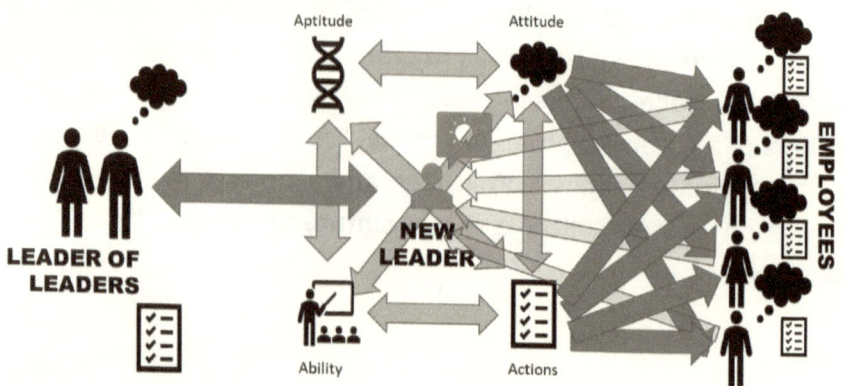

...the culture (abilities, aptitudes, and actions) of the organization tend to force that element into back into the same culturally acceptable attitudes, aptitudes, and actions... or the foreign element is removed.

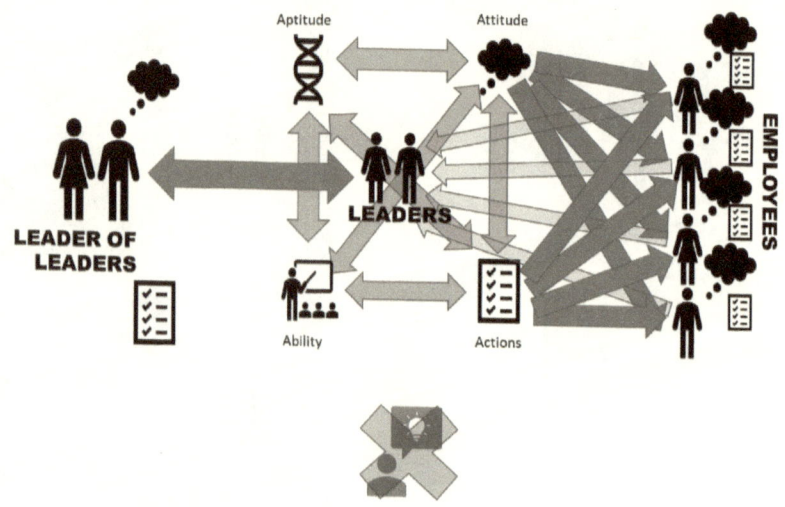

Now, let's practice dissecting the systems by revising the war stories.

CHAPTER 6: DISSECTING THE WAR STORIES

"The people don't run the system; the people are victims of the system."
– Ziggy Marley

We've established that leadership consists of four-A's: Attitude, Aptitude, Abilities, and Actions. We see examples of these four-A's in each of the war stories as well as the interdependence between these four-As. Let's spend some time reviewing the war stories again. This time let's turn the war stories into case studies by examining them with a critical eye using the framework of the four A's: attitudes, aptitudes, abilities, and actions.

CASE STUDY: ABE, THE AMATEUR

Abe showed an **aptitude** for being bright, ambitious, charismatic that produced **actions** of working overtime, asking for extra responsibilities, and studying. By studying policy manuals and test books, Abe gained managerial **abilities**. These actions resulted in a promotion.

The promotion reinforced Abe's **attitude** about hard work, resulting in more **actions** of hard work. These actions resulted in another promotion.

On his own, Abe's **attitude** was the only thing that mattered was hard work. Although the team at Abe's branch were all more experienced than Abe, the company's **action** (promoting him because of his hard work) further reinforcing Abe's **attitude**.

Abe's **attitude** led to the **action** of criticizing his employees. The HQ's **actions** (ignoring complaints) reinforced Abe's **attitude**.

As things went bad (employees leaving, poor customer service scores, and lower operational performance), Abe continued doing the **actions** (hard work) that had led his to prior success: he worked long hours, seven days a week.

Then Abe did an **action** (brought people with the same **attitude** -- relatives who were hard workers). The success of this **action** created the **attitude** that it was okay to bend the rules. To continue his **action** (hard work), Abe bent more the rules (another **action**). He knew this action was wrong but justified his **actions** based on his **attitude** of hard work. Ultimately, Abe's actions resulted in consequences.

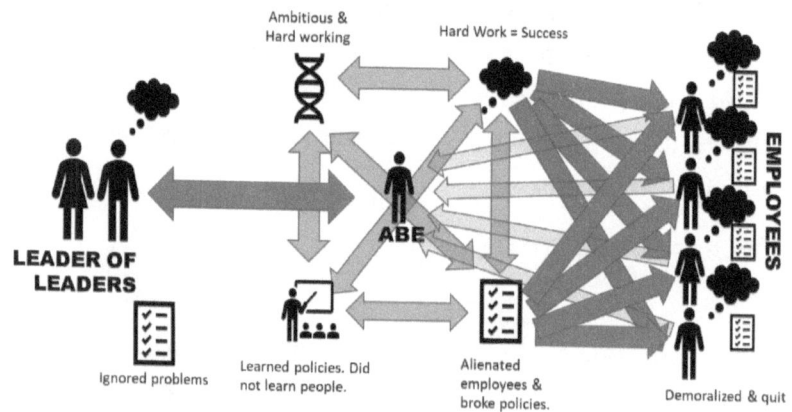

The interaction of the 4As with Abe.

CASE STUDY: BARELY-THERE-BECKI

Becki had an **aptitude** for consistency, resulting in the **action** of staying with the company for a long time. That **action** led to **abilities** to run the department, which led to a promotion.

The **actions** of Becki's team and company led to an **attitude** of not feeling like she needed to be there, which led to the actions of skipping out of work. The **actions** of the company reinforced Becki's **attitude**. This growing **attitude** leads to more inappropriate **actions**, calling in sick and sleeping at work.

The **action** (or lack of action) by the company creates an **attitude** among Becki's employees that it was okay to skip work, which leads to **actions** of taking long lunches, covering for one another, and falsifying timesheets.

Ultimately these **actions** resulted in negative consequences for Becki.

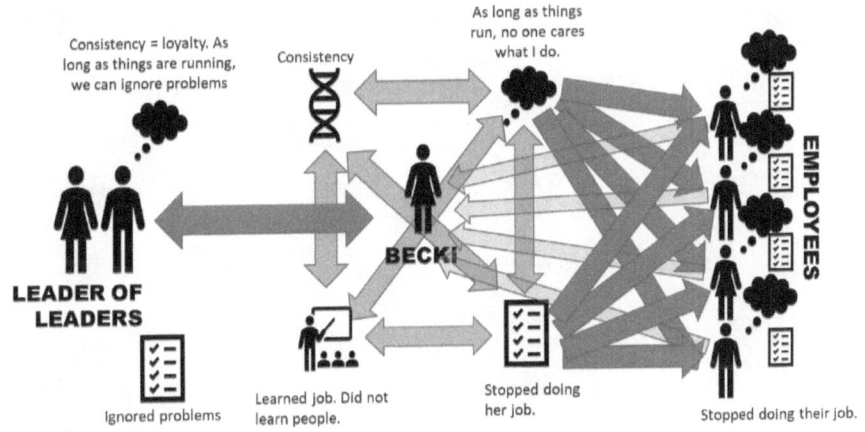

The interaction of the 4As with Becki

Case Study: Complaining Clyde

Clyde had engineering **abilities**, skills he had to learn through his training, which resulted in an **attitude** that his abilities were valuable. The **actions** of the company during the hiring process reinforced that **attitude**. Clyde also had the **attitude** that expectations, performance, and tools should be the same quality as a large engineering company. He had the **attitude** that productivity was the result of tools and skills. He had the **attitude** that his experience at large companies should give him credibility in the new organization.

Clyde's **attitudes** led to the **action** of asking for more resources. The company had the **attitude** that hard work was more important than tools and skills. These conflicting attitudes were the first signs of cultural misalignment. Clyde believed that everyone in the company had the same **attitude** regarding tools and training and that the lack of resources was a result of not understanding the terrible conditions. This caused the **action** of complaining.

Ultimately, Clyde's **actions** led to the consequence of termination.

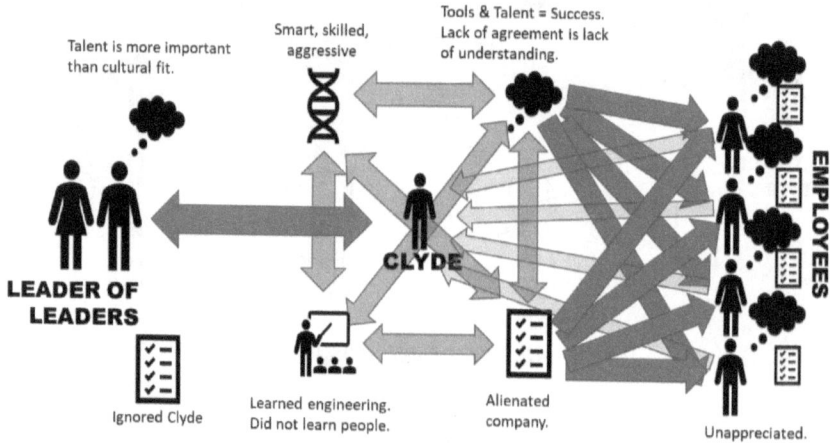

The interaction of the 4As with Clyde

CASE STUDY: DOUG DEALS WITH THE DEMORALIZED

The **actions** of the former manager had caused the team to believe (**attitude**) that the manager made unrealistic demands and forced them to work 60-hours a week.

Doug demonstrated the skill (**ability**) to assess the situation. Doug did not have technical **abilities**, but he believed (**attitude**) that he could trust the team if he could overcome their negative **attitude**.

Doug used **actions** to communicate that he was different, including individual meetings, listening, reassuring the staff that he was there to help, and extending trust.

Doug then applied his **ability** to assess situations to make a plan (**action**). Doug confronted Joe (an **action**). Doug believed (**attitude**) that he could turn Joe around.

Doug's **action** and Joe's **attitude** about changing led to him quitting (**action**). Doug believed (**attitude**) he had personal responsibility for Joe's **actions**.

Again, we see Doug using his **ability** of situational assessment to get some extra budget for the team and spent that money on training his team (**actions**). Those **actions** demonstrate Doug's **attitude** of caring. Doug was using **actions** needed to overcome the team's **attitude** that they were only there to do a job. Doug's <u>consistent</u> **actions** and **attitude** over time resulted in changing the team's **attitude** and **actions**.

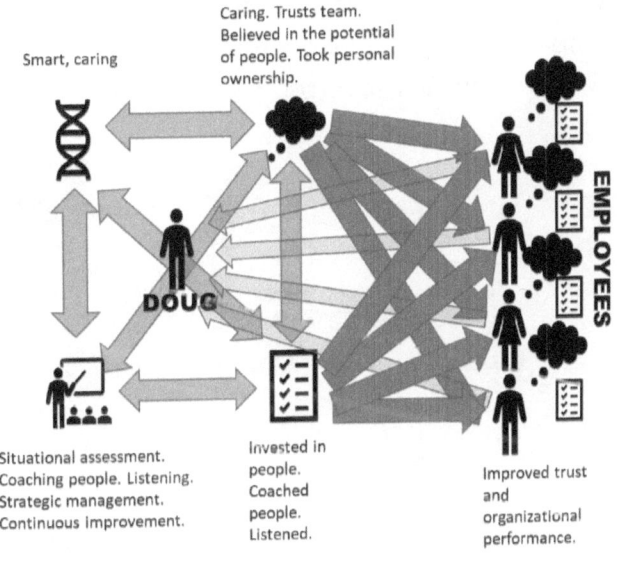

Caring. Trusts team. Believed in the potential of people. Took personal ownership.

Smart, caring

EMPLOYEES

DOUG

Situational assessment. Coaching people. Listening. Strategic management. Continuous improvement.

Invested in people. Coached people. Listened.

Improved trust and organizational performance.

The interaction of the 4As with Doug.

Case Study: Emailing Elle

Let's start with Ian. Ian was humble; he had an **attitude** that he didn't know everything. We can also see Ian's **attitude** toward education by considering an MBA. These **attitudes** led to the **action** of asking Elle for her advice.

Elle had an **attitude** that she should help people. That **attitude** led her to the **action** of agreeing to talk to Ian. During the talk, Elle demonstrated **actions** of listening and advising, which came from her **ability** to mentor.

Elle continued to use her **ability** to mentor to grow Ian into a leader. These actions led to Ian getting promoted. Ian's **actions** as a leader reflected the **attitude** that he learned from Elle's **attitude**.

Elle's attitude led to **actions** to help Ian continue to advance. Her consistent **actions** led Ian to have an **attitude** of trust. Ian's grateful **attitude** led him to the **action** of working hard. This action, in turn, led to more promotions, which reinforced his **actions** and **attitudes**.

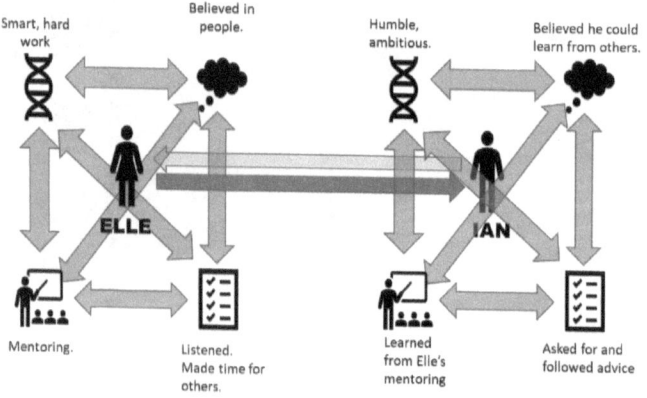

The interaction of the 4As with Elle & Ian.

CASE STUDY: FIX-IT-FRED

Because of Fred's past success (**actions**), Fred believed (**attitude**) that he could turn around this poor performing organizations. Fred applied his skills (**abilities**) of strategic management and process improvement, Fred took **actions** which resulted in consequences: the company became a profitable organization. The success of his **abilities** and the praise (action) of the President reinforced Fred's **attitude**.

Fred continued to apply his **abilities** to improve the organization. However, the President of the company stopped providing guidance and changed his behavior to complaining (**actions**).

When Fred attempted to continue his **actions**, he faced resistance and criticism (**actions**) by the President. The President shifted his **actions** from praise to criticism.

The shifting **actions** of the President caused Fred frustration. Fred turned to his historically successful **ability** of strategic management and process improvement to create a plan (**action**). The President continued to resist (**action**), which ultimately resulted in the consequence of Fred being removed a month later.

CASE STUDY: GRACE'S GAMES

Full disclosure: I was Harold in this war story. My peers and I all knew that we were competing for the same job. We compared notes over lunch during the interview and we had all agreed that we would be comfortable working for one another. It would sting, but I trusted those guys. I had an **attitude** of trust based on our time together and their consistent **actions** during our time together. I believe they had the same. Grace was definitely not this person's name, but the information in the story was absolutely true. Grace was the worse boss I ever worked for.

Grace definitely had interviewing **ability** (skill). I was impressed initially; however, her interview **abilities** did <u>not</u> align with her **attitude** or **her actions**, which resulted in the sense that something was wrong.

Grace really never attempted to learn anything about us. She would have quickly learned that the three of us had a close relationship and her actions wouldn't work.

Grace believed (**attitude**) that isolation and rivalry led to increased performance. That **attitude** led her to separate the three of us and tell us each different information (**actions**). Fortunately, my peers and I had an **attitude** of solidarity that led to **actions** of resisting. The failure of Grace's **actions** resulted in her micromanaging behaviors (**actions**).

Grace's **ability** to charm people resulted in changing the reporting solution.

I have a skill (**ability**) to understanding people and their motivations. It's an **ability** that I developed from years of studying people (**action**) and reading books on human behavior. I didn't understand Grace's attitude or behavior, and I started investigating (**action**) Grace. I believed (**attitude**) if I understood her better, I could work better with her.

I'm very active on LinkedIn (**ability**). When I looked at Grace's LinkedIn profile, I found out that I was connected to Grace's old boss. I asked him out to lunch (**action**) to learn more about Grace. That's when he said, "Good luck. She's a piece of work" and told me about Grace's political maneuvering (**ability**) and backstabbing that led to Grace's entire team quitting at his company. Candidly, I panicked at this.

I believe (**attitude**) in the value of mentoring. When I was trying to get the job, I had established a mentoring relationship (**action**) with Michael, Grace's soon-to-be boss. Michael and I had a good relationship and I believed (**attitude**) he should know about Grace's history. Plus, I hated Grace for her deception and attempting to create division between my friends.

Michael did the right thing. He supported his employee, Grace. I think he was in a no-win situation. I suspect Michael talked to Grace and tried to correct her behavior, but I don't know that for sure.

Grace believed (**attitude**) I was a threat, which led to the action of trying to replace me. Fortunately, my team knows that I am fiercely loyal to them and her attempts fell flat.

Because I believed (**attitude**) Grace was a liar and would deny anything, I recorded her (**action**). I also believe in being painfully honest (**attitude**), which led to the **action** of confronting Grace.

Because my **attitudes** were so far out of alignment with Grace's **attitudes**, I left, the entire team followed, as did Thomas and Richard.

Case Study: Making a List, Checking It Twice

Hans' belief (**attitude**) that activity was the same as value led to the belief (**attitude**) that he needed to know everything that was happening in the department led to the **action** of meetings every Monday with his employees. This **action** created an **attitude** in the team that they needed to justify their existence. It led to avoidance

actions from those who didn't believe (**attitude**) the meeting had value.

How about your story? What attitudes were present? What aptitudes? How about actions? How did they interact? Learning to identify the 4As influencing your environment will help develop your systems-thinking abilities. Write down the 4As that you identified.

_____ lead to _____.

_____ lead to _____.

_____ lead to _____.

_____ lead to _____.

_____ lead to _____.

SECTION 2 – BECOMING A GREAT LEADER

CHAPTER 7: D-K MEASURING

"I am, as I've said, merely competent. But in an age of incompetence, that makes me extraordinary." – Billy Joel

There was this great movie in the late eighties: Funny Farm. Chevy Chase and Madolyn Smith bought a country home in a little town of Redbud. Chase was trying to get away to write a novel. Comedy ensues. It's weird how many comedies include authors trying to get away to finish their novel. Funny Farm, As Good As It Gets, The Shining, Misery... Maybe I'll finish this book at an abandoned hotel... seems like a good idea...

Anyway, Funny Farm... while the movers are trying to find the road that the home is on, the gas station attendant, Mac, gives them some convoluted directions which result in them attempting to drive a massive semi across a rickety wooden bridge. At one point during the instructions, Mac says, "If I was going to Dog Creek Road, I sure as hell wouldn't start from here."

The moral of this story is you need to know where you are to get where you are going.

SELF-ASSESSMENT

Self-assessment is very dangerous. Human beings are fraught with subconscious biases that make measuring their own performance accurately. Fortunately, I've devised a way to turn that weakness into a strength.

Here are two quick and easy questions that can honestly assess your leadership skills. It's straight from my first book *UNF*CK IT!*

Don't look ahead yet. If you look ahead, you don't honestly want to know what kind of leader you really are. Answer these two short questions:

I think great leadership is:

(A) Pretty easy
(B) Not too hard
(C) Very hard
(D) Nearly impossible

As a leader I am/would be:

(A) Trying my best
(B) Average
(C) Above average
(D) Pretty good

Write down your answers before looking ahead.

Psychologists found an interesting cognitive bias called the Dunning-Kruger (D-K) effect. It basically looks like this:

- If you don't know anything about something, you probably think it's pretty easy and you'd be pretty good at it.
- If you know a little bit about something, you probably think it's not too hard, but that you are probably above average.
- If you know a good amount about something, you might realize it's ridiculously hard and that you suck.
- If you know a ton about something, you usually realize it's almost impossible and that you are just learning.

Now, look at your answers from the previous page. Give yourself points like this:

I think great leadership is:

As a leader I am/would be:

0 points for (A) Pretty easy
1 point for (B) Not too hard
2 points for (C) Very hard
3 points for (D) Nearly impossible

3 points for (A) Trying my best
2 points for (B) Average
1 point for (C) Above average
0 points for (D) Pretty good

Score:

0 – 1 You might want to forget everything you think you know about being a leader. Someone might have recommended this book to you. Hell, they might have slipped it into your inbox. They are trying to tell you something, but are too scared to do it. Really. I'm hardcore glad you are reading this.

2 – 3 Don't worry. The research shows that most people think they are above average. The math shows they are wrong. If the average is 50% by the definition of 50%, half the people are below average. Most of those people think they are above average. Those people are wrong. You are one of those people. I'm happy you're reading this book.

4 – 5 You actually know enough about leadership to know that you don't know much about leadership. I love people like you. You are probably more practiced than most leaders and you still bought this book to get better. Impressive.

6 Very likely you have been leading a while. You know this job is the hardest thing that you've done or ever will do. Join the club. Thanks for reading this. I'd like to meet you. I'll bet we'd be great friends.

GETTING FEEDBACK

Another method of assessing your leadership skills is to ask. The problem is that most people do not provide accurate feedback, particularly negative and almost never to their leaders.

That's a real problem.

I have a hard time getting honest feedback from my team. Most leaders do. I've found that most people who I lead are afraid that honest critical feedback will lead to retribution, or that I don't want to hear what they think, or that they are not in a position to judge me. But leaders *need* feedback. Leading without feedback is like driving blindfolded.

One afternoon during a performance review with a software development supervisor who reported to me, we had completed my feedback discussion with him and were going through my rote request for feedback,

> Me: "How can I do better?"
>
> Him: "You're great. The best leader I ever had."

Me: "I can't do anything better?"

Him: "I can't think of anything."

Me: *Sigh.*

This supervisor didn't know what to measure. He didn't know what I do day-to-day. He was thinking about his former bosses and comparing me with them because that's all he ever knew. But *I didn't want to be better than them; I want to be the best version of myself.*

> Me: "I don't write a line of code. Not one. I don't gather user specifications, write unit tests, define sprints, hold stand-ups, groom backlogs. In fact, I don't do anything that makes Nucor one dime. Did you know that? **All I do is make you and your team more or less productive.** That's it. If I make you more productive, the company makes more money. If I make you less productive, I make the company less money."

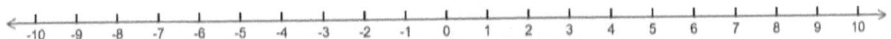

> I continued, "So imagine a scale -10 to +10. At zero, I have no impact on your productivity at all. I make your team no better or no worse. At +10, everything I do makes you and your team more productive. At -10, everything I do makes you and your team less productive. Now I like to think I'm a positive number, maybe a 2... maybe a 3... but hell, I could be a 0 or a -5. You tell me. What number would you give me?"

> He thought for a minute and said, "A six or a seven."

> "Wow. That's generous. Thanks. Let's call it a 7. I want to be 8 next year. How do I get to 8?"

He said immediately, "I wish you would stick to your schedule for our leadership training. It gets rescheduled all the time. I prepare for the meeting and you have to reschedule."

"You're right. I do that. I'll do better. Thanks."

The Two Questions

I was so happy with the specific feedback that I've incorporated these two questions into all my review sessions. This formula results in specific action items that you can immediately apply to become a better leader.

> Question #1: "Imagine a scale -10 to +10. At zero, I have no impact on your productivity at all. I make your job and your team no better or no worse. At +10, _everything_ I do makes you and your team more productive. At -10, _everything_ I do makes you and your team less productive. What number would you give me?"

> Question #2: "I want to be X+1 next year. How do I get to X+1?"

This is a risky set of questions. It's risky because you might hear that you are a zero... or worse. It's risky because you <u>will</u> get feedback and your team will watch to see if you incorporate it. **But you have to decide if it's riskier to take the blindfold off or keep driving.**

By the way, I know this works because one of my supervisors came up to me afterward and said, "I started using your -10 to +10 scale with my team during reviews. I've been getting great feedback."

CHAPTER 8: SHOW ME YOUR AS

"Role-playing games are just an organic improvised space for storytelling." – Matthew Mercer

I'd like to thank the Duffer Brothers for the resurgence of Dungeons & Dragons. I played a ton of TSR's Advanced Dungeons & Dragons 3rd Edition during the 80s. Now it's cool again... or just cool... the "again" implies it was cool before. It was not. Really. I was a pimply-faced, fat, card-carrying Mensa-member, computer geek who played Dungeons & Dragons. As you can imagine, I had to fight off the babes...

I have no idea how I ended up with my sexy wife. I imagine some Divine Dungeon Master rolling his eyes and saying, "OK... you can try to meet the hot chick, but you're gonna need a really high roll..."

Holy Shit!

When you start a role-playing game, you fill out a character sheet with your character's stats, a numeric representation of how strong they are, how smart, how charming, etc... Almost like the character's **aptitudes**. You also list the skills they have – much like **abilities**. These stats and skills control what you do during a game or their **actions**.

That's what we are doing now. We determined your current leadership skill level in the previous chapter. Now we are going to look at your aptitudes and then your abilities. We are making a character sheet for you. I've put a character sheet blank in the appendix. (You have my written permission to make copies of the character sheet on page 133 for personal, non-commercial use. You may not distribute these sheets online or in any digital form.)

HA! Now you're a role-playing nerd too...

This is an important step in leadership growth. It's called an **assessment**. Leaders who conduct an assessment prior to taking leadership training are far more likely to be successful than leaders who don't. Besides that, we made a sacred pact, so do the fucking work.

We've talked at length about the 4As. Let's define your natural aptitudes. Things you have a natural tendency to be good at or not so good:

Here's a very basic, non-comprehensive list of aptitudes. The ones in bold are aptitudes mentioned in the War Stories in Chapter 3. Feel free to add to this list:

Adaptable	Empathetic	Innovative	Sensible
Ambitious	Encouraging	Listener	Serious
Approachable	Enthusiastic	Loyal	Silly
Authentic	Focused	Merciful	Stable
Brave	Generous	Modest	Tolerant
Bright	Grateful	Nice	Trusting

Calm	Happy	Optimistic	Truthful
Charismatic	Humble	Persistent	Unbiased
Considerate	Humorous	Planner	Understanding
Consistency	Imaginative	Polite	Unselfish
Cooperative	Independent	Positive	_____
Decisive	Industrious	Resilient	_____

Let's add the aptitudes to your "character sheet". Circle the aptitudes that you feel strongly identify you. Some people might look at the list and say, "Adaptable… yup, that's me. Ambitious… me. Approachable… me. Authentic… also me. Brave, bright, calm… me, me, me. Damn. I'm amazing." I'm limiting you to five choices. Pick the aptitude that most defines you. Then from the remaining aptitudes pick the next aptitude that most defines you. Wash, rinse, repeat.

If you are having trouble identifying your aptitudes, call your mom. Ask her what you were like as a child.

Hell… call your mom anyway. She misses you. I'll be right back. I need to call my mom.

OK... I'm back...Let's continue filling out your character sheet.

We've assessed your aptitudes. Let's look at abilities. Remember, abilities are acquired talents, something that you can learn. Abilities can be acquired through formal training, self-education, modeling, mentoring, coaching, or the school of hard knocks.

Let's look at some common leader skills:

COMMUNICATION SKILLS

Communicating is a learned skill. Do you know how I know? Let's try an experiment. Hand this book to a three-month-old. Ask them what I mean when I say, "unfuck leadership." They didn't understand? Why not? Oh.... They haven't <u>learned</u> to read a book or understand you?

(Did you seriously just say, "unfuck" to a three-month-old? You need some professional help, mate.)

Seriously, dude.

Common communication skills include:

Active listening	Presentation & Public Speaking
Clarifying and explaining	Reading Body Language
Nonverbal communication	Storytelling
Clear, concise, coherent	

communication

MOTIVATION SKILLS

A leader needs to be able to motivate people to accomplish goals. Great leaders accomplish goals through other people. Motivation is also a teachable skill.

Some common motivational skills include:

Understanding Other's Interests	Providing Autonomy
Demonstrating Gratitude	Providing Challenging Work
Demonstrating Trust	Recognizing and Rewarding Employees
Goal Setting	Team-building

DELEGATION SKILLS

Delegation is another tool that leaders learn. Giving your followers tasks, defining the desired outcomes, and ensuring the work is completed in an important part of leading. These delegation skills are some of the tools that will help you do this:

Allocating Resources	Identifying Measurable Outcomes
Evaluating Outcomes	Matching the Task to the Right Person
Following-Up	Setting & Communicating Expectations

TRUST-BUILDING SKILLS

"You can have some amazing vision... but if you don't have the hearts & minds of your employees... you just shouldn't be in leadership." – David Rettig, Sync Magazine, October 2017

Common trust-building skills that a leader may use:

Consistency	Honesty
Doing the Right Thing	Integrity
Empathy	Maintaining Confidence
Extend Trust	Transparency

DEVELOPING OTHER PEOPLE SKILLS

The best leaders develop other people. Whenever I start in a new organization, I recite Donald Rumsfeld's quote: "You go to war with the army you have, not the army you might want or wish to have..." As a leader, your army is your team, the people would follow you. If you don't have the army you want, it's your responsibility to grow them into the army you need.

Assessing Strengths (& Weaknesses)	Follow up
Encouraging	Providing Feedback
Training	

COMMITMENT SKILLS

Your team's maximum commitment will be exactly as committed as you are. Not one iota more (and quite possibly less). When things get tough, you won't back down. No, you won't back down. You could stand up at the gates of hell and you'll stand your ground

Alignment with Company Priorities	Perseverance
Determination	Reliability
Embracing your development	Thoroughness
Passion	

ORGANIZATIONAL SKILLS

Although organizational skills are usually associated with management rather than leadership based on the Day delineation, leaders may have training in these common skills:

Financial Management	Project planning
Meeting Management	Strategic Planning
Prioritizing Tasks	Time management

The last three skills might raise some hackles. Some people will argue that creativity, risk-taking, and thinking are not skills, but are inborn. Many intelligent people would argue that these are some divine spark or genetics. These people often consider themselves very intelligent, very creative, or very risktakery... I guess that's not a word.

Let's start with risk-taking. Can I train you not to take risks?

Imagine you have a new idea at your job. It will cost $10,000, but there's a 50-50 chance that it would net your company $1,000,000. You run it by your boss. She jumps on it. The risk is low and the upside is amazing. But, like ideas sometimes do, the plan fails. Your company loses $10,000. Not a big sum for your company, but your boss publicly calls you on the carpet. She berates you for wasting the company's money, her time, and her political capital. She questions your intelligence. She asks if you don't have enough work to do since you have time to chase harebrained schemes.

A month later, you have another idea. Are you more or less likely to take the risk? Obviously, your boss **trained you to be less risk-taking**.

Let's rewind. Imagine you have a new idea at your job. It will cost $10,000, but there's a 50-50 chance that it would net your company $1,000,000. You run it by your boss. She jumps on it. The risk is low and the upside is amazing. But, like ideas sometimes do, the plan fails. Your company loses $10,000. Not a big sum for your company. Your boss brings up your failed idea during a big company meeting and says, "This is exactly the kind of out-of-the-box thinking we need. I love that [your name] shared this idea. This is the kind of experimental ideas that we love to try. Even if it didn't work out, it showed the kind of leadership that we need."

A month later, you have another idea. Are you going to present it? Absolutely. **Because your boss trained you to take risks.**

RISK-TAKING SKILLS

Courage	Improvising
Decision Making	Initiative
Forecasting	Judgment

CREATIVITY SKILLS

Okay... you think. Maybe risk-taking is trainable.

But creativity is different. Creativity comes from magic rainbow beams that dump into ideas into people's brains... However, the elements of creativity are trainable. The skills that increase the likelihood of inspiration are trainable.

Let me give you another example: give me a creative idea for the application of quantum cryptography for the country of Tuvalu's economics. Go ahead. Write down your actionable, creative idea for implementing quantum cryptography in Tuvalu to help its economy. I can wait...

What? You don't have an idea? Why? You don't have training in quantum cryptography? You had to read a Wikipedia article to figure it out and you're still not sure?

Furthermore, you don't know anything about Tuvalu or its economy. You actually had to look up Tuvalu to find out if it's a real place?

Do you know what helps general creative solutions? Curiosity about a subject. Curiosity leads to research and learning. Broad knowledge about subjects leads to identifying patterns in those subjects, conceptualization about those subjects, and synthesizing concepts from different arenas into new ideas. Open-mindedness to new ideas and listening to others' ideas about subjects. All of these are trainable.

Curiosity
Open-mindedness
Listening to others' ideas
Identifying patterns

Making abstract connections
Synthesizing
Conceptualization

THINKING SKILLS

Lastly thinking skills are trainable. There are a number of great books that talk about growing your thinking skills. A few of my favorites are De Bono's *Six Thinking Hats*, Kahneman's *Thinking, Fast and Slow,* and anything on Bloom's taxonomy.

Analysis
Cognitive Flexibility
Critical Thinking
Emotional Intelligence

Logical
Organized
Problem-solving

YOUR CHARACTER SHEET

Which of these abilities have you been trained in, either formally or informally? Don't list the abilities that you *think* you have. List the abilities that you've been trained in. Training could be in a classroom, reading books, formal or informal mentoring, or intentionally modeling the behavior of a leader you admire. The qualifier is intentional. This is something that you tried to learn. Not something that you *think* you do.

List up to five abilities that you've received the <u>most</u> training in on your character sheet.

Now list the other abilities that you have <u>any</u> training in.

ATTITUDES

Attitudes are the beliefs that a leader holds about themselves and others. Attitudes may not be rational. I'm dedicating the entire next chapter to attitude because it's a little long.

CHAPTER 9: LET ME ASK YOU SOMETHING

"I have no special talents. I am only passionately curious." – *Albert Einstein*

Remember that attitudes are the beliefs that a leader holds about themselves and others. Attitudes may not be rational. In this section, we will ask some questions about your attitudes. Answer honestly. There's not a right or wrong answer. No one is going to see your answers (unless you fill this out and share the book. And don't do that. Make them buy their own copy. The author has bills to pay.)

ATTITUDE QUESTIONS

1.	People work hardest when watched.	T	F
2.	Higher education is important.	T	F
3.	People will twist the facts to their advantage.	T	F
4.	Direction is set by the team.	T	F
5.	People want to be told what to do.	T	F
6.	People should be grateful for a job.	T	F
7.	People need a pat on the back.	T	F
8.	People willingly follow me.	T	F
9.	I know more than most people.	T	F
10.	Having the title of a leader is important to lead.	T	F
11.	What I do is more important than what I say.	T	F
12.	Information is shared on a "need to know" basis.	T	F
13.	My boss decides how well I'm doing my job.	T	F
14.	The company will give me the training I need.	T	F
15.	It's easy to help find areas for others to improve.	T	F
16.	Competition helps improve performance.	T	F
17.	I worry that my team makes me look bad.	T	F
18.	I don't care about office politics.	T	F
19.	I hold people accountable for their failures.	T	F

20. My personal issues do not affect my work.   T   F
21. Having friends at work isn't too important   T   F
22. The devil is in the details   T   F
23. Some people just shouldn't lead. Ever.   T   F
24. Problems today are more important tomorrow's.   T   F
25. People don't change.   T   F
26. Some people are better at leading.   T   F
27. Training/conferences provide a break from work.   T   F
28. I don't like to take credit that I'm due.   T   F
29. Work isn't fun.   T   F
30. The big picture is important.   T   F
31. Change is important.   T   F
32. Maintaining the status quo is important.   T   F
33. I'm too busy to plan.   T   F
34. I wish my employees would do what I said.   T   F
35. People understand me.   T   F
36. I'm not charismatic.   T   F
37. I hate giving negative feedback.   T   F
38. My boss does not want my feedback.   T   F
39. It's important that my team get along.   T   F
40. I drive results.   T   F
41. Sometimes a leader should just make a decision.   T   F
42. Leaders deserve trust.   T   F
43. Leaders need to be experts in their area.   T   F
44. People need to have a say in what they do.   T   F
45. Listening to others' opinions is important.   T   F
46. I like to have all the facts before deciding.   T   F
47. Employees want to be left alone to do their job.   T   F
48. I don't like to ask for help.   T   F
49. My team has everything they need to do their job.   T   F
50. Training should be relevant to the current job.   T   F
51. You should celebrate team wins.   T   F
52. Celebrating individuals might create rivalry.   T   F

Answer key: *There is no answer key.* Because there are no right or wrong answers. The questions were to engage your brain and help you identify some of your attitudes.

> "Everyone is necessarily the hero of his own life story."
>
> John Barth, *Esquire Magazine,* 1958

Every answer represents two sides of a coin. Let's look at each question and both sides of the coin. With each, ask yourself if any of these ring true. Now, no one ever imagines they are the bad guy. They justify their behavior and, if they do recognize that they did something "questionable", they explain that away as the result of circumstance. This self-justification is one part of the fundamental attribution error. Therefore, if something *could* be true for you or if anyone has *ever* said this to you (even if you don't believe it), mark it.

Q1: People work hardest when watched.

- ☐ If you answered true, you *might* be micromanaging. You might not trust people.
- ☐ If you answered false, you *might* not be following-up on your team. You might be too trusting.

Q2: Higher education is important.

- ☐ If you answered true, you *might* overvalue education. You might miss a great candidate without a degree. You *might* promote people based on education rather than performance.

91

- ☐ If you answered false, you *might* not consider going back to school to gain new abilities. You *might* not encourage people to grow through higher education. You *might* dismiss educated people as academics (Trust me, insecure managers have dismissed my professional experience because I am educated.

Q3: People will twist the facts to their advantage.

- ☐ If you answered true, you *might* not trust people.
- ☐ If you answered false, you *might* be too trusting.

Q4: Direction is set by the team.

Teams need direction. Some leaders prefer to allow teams to set their own direction. Some leaders may set the direction for the team.

- ☐ True might indicate that you empower your team. If might indicate trust. However, take to the extreme, you could be viewed as having abdicated your responsibilities are a leader. You could also be seen as indecisive.
- ☐ False might It might indicate that you fail to empower your team. You may micromanage the team. You might not trust your team.

Q5: People want to be told what to do.

Again, people want to clearly understand your expectations for them; however, they also want autonomy (the ability to control their own actions). As a leader, you need to balance those.

- ☐ True might indicate too much reliance on direction rather than empowering. If could indicate a tendency to micromanage and a lack of trust.
- ☐ False could indicate a lack of clear expectations or too much latitude. You may trust your team too much. You may fail to communicate your expectations.

Q6: People should be grateful for a job.

Gratitude is important; however, expecting gratitude from people might be founded on some unhealthy attitudes or lead to unhealthy behavior.

- ☐ True might mean that you don't recognize your employees for their work. You might need to publicly and privately praise your employees more.
- ☐ False could mean that you don't drive your employees sufficiently. You might have a tendency to see the positive and miss the negative. You might fail to hold people to a high standard.

Q7: People need a pat on the back.

- ☐ True could mean that you aren't driving your employees enough.
- ☐ False could mean that you don't recognize your employees enough.

Q8: People willingly follow me.

- ☐ True may mean that you rely too much on referent power.
- ☐ False may mean that you need to develop your referent power.

Q9: I know more than most people.

- ☐ If you said true, you might rely too much on expert power. You may need to develop other forms of influence. People might have accused you of "needing to be the smartest person in the room." You might fail to seek the opinions of others.
- ☐ If you said false,

Q10: Having the title of a leader is important to lead.

The title of the leader confers positional power. However, you don't want to rely exclusively on positional power.

- ☐ If you answered true, you may be overly dependent on your title to lead.
- ☐ If you answered false, you may not be using your positional-power fully.

Q11: What I do is more important than what I say

- ☐ A true answer may indicate a tendency to fail to communicate regularly, consistently, or clearly.
- ☐ A false answer may indicate a failure to model appropriate actions. Modeling behavior is an important part of transformational leadership.

Q12: Information is shared on a "need to know" basis.

- ☐ Information transparency creates trust, creates employee empowerment, and improves innovation. If you answered true, you may be missing opportunities to increase trust, employee engagement, and innovation.
- ☐ If you answered false, oversharing can creates distractions.

Q13: My boss decides how well I'm doing my job.

- ☐ If you answered true, you might undervalue feedback from peers or subordinates. You might also be looking for validation from your boss rather than striving to improve because of the intrinsic value of self-improvement.
- ☐ If you answered false, you might not fully understand the importance of office politics and feedback from your boss.

Q14: The company will give me the training I need.

- ☐ If you answered true, you may fail to take ownership of your own development. You may expect others to train you and develop you. You might undervalue the importance of training.
- ☐ If you answered false, you might be missing training opportunities because your company does not offer training.

Q15: It's easy to help find areas for others to improve.

- ☐ People who answer true might be seen as hypercritical of others.
- ☐ A false answer may indicate a failure to provide constructive feedback that could help others improve. It could also indicate a desire to avoid conflict.

Q16: Competition helps improve performance.

- ☐ If you answered true, you may be overly competitive and underestimate the value of collaboration.
- ☐ If you answered false, you may underestimate the value of competition and may avoid conflict.

Q17: I worry that my team makes me look bad.

- ☐ A true answer could indicate a tendency to need to be liked. It could indicate a failure to take ownership of a problem. It could indicate a failure to address performance problems on your team.
- ☐ A false answer could indicate a lack of awareness of office politics.

Q18: I don't care about office politics.

- ☐ If you answered true, you may not be fully taking advantage of politics as a vehicle for influence.
- ☐ If you answered false, you might be overly influenced by office politics.

Q19: I hold people accountable for their failures.

Earlier we read about the fundamental attribution error. Fundamental attribution error is why we blame people for their mistakes but excuse our own. For example, if we get caught speeding, we were in a hurry to get to work or we weren't paying attention, but if someone else gets a speeding ticket, they are reckless.

- □ If you answered true to holding people accountable, you might be a victim of fundamental attribution error. You might be blaming people for things that were really just an accident. You might be training people to not take risks. You might be reducing innovation. You might be hyper-critical. You might be avoiding your part in the failure.
- □ If you answered false, you might be excusing failures. You might not be holding people to a high enough standard.

Q20: My personal issues do not affect my work.

- □ A true answer might indicate unrealistic expectations for employees and failure to recognize a holistic view of people. You may not demonstrate a genuine interest in others.
- □ A false answer might indicate a failure to hold yourself or others to high enough performance standards.

Q21: Having friends at work isn't too important

- □ If you say true, you might underestimate the effect of friends in the workplace. People who have friends at work are less likely to turn over (quit) and more likely to be high performers. Do you want high performers who don't quit?
- □ If you say false, you could be perceived as too social and not driven enough.

Q22: The devil is in the details

- □ A true answer may indicate a propensity to micromanage people. Sometimes people who gather a lot of details are perceived as overly analytical and afraid to make a decision.
- □ A false answer might indicate a lack of attention to details.

Q23: Some people just shouldn't lead. Ever.

- □ If you indicated true, you may fail to invest in or train people who don't meet your preconceived definition of a leader. You may also only promote people who meet your preconceived ideas. The answer could indicate a lack of diversity of background or perspective on your leadership team.

☐ If you indicated false, you may be overly optimistic about people and fail to honestly assess their leadership skills.

Q24: Problems today are more important tomorrow's.

☐ Focusing on immediate problems can lead to firefighters' syndrome, where the excitement of dealing with urgency becomes a reinforcer for dealing with urgent problems only. I talk at length about firefighter's syndrome in *UNF*CK IT!* Focusing on the immediate issues may result in a lack of strategic focus and lack of proactive thought leadership

☐ If one fails to address immediate problems, some might see this as a lack of action or an inability to address the immediate needs of the business.

Q25: People don't change.

☐ If you believe that people don't change, you may fail to invest in others and may fail to invest in your own personal development. If you believe that people generally don't change, your attitude may reinforce unwanted actions in others, rather than improving behavior.

☐ If you believe that people are capable of change, you might become critical of those who don't change. You may overlook negatives behaviors or attitudes, hoping they will change in the future.

Q26: Some people are better at leading.

☐ If you indicated true, you may fail to invest in or train people who don't meet your preconceived definition of a leader. You may also only promote people who meet your preconceived ideas. The answer could indicate a lack of diversity of background or perspective on your leadership team.

- ☐ If you indicated false, you may be overly optimistic about people and fail to honestly assess their leadership skills.

Q27: Training/conferences provide a break from work.

- ☐ Some people falsely believe that training and conferences are merely excuses to avoid work. If you believe that, you might fail to take advantage of the high-quality training available.
- ☐ However, if you answered false, you may fail to properly vet training and conference requests. You may also fail to hold people accountable for sharing the value that they receive from conferences.

Q28: I don't like to take credit that I'm due.

- ☐ If you answered true, you may be missing opportunities to gain political capital. Leadership requires the accumulation of influence and accepting the credit that you are due is part of accumulating influence.
- ☐ If you answered false, you might need to check that you are also giving credit to your team. It's easy to fall into the habit of accepting the credit without acknowledging the importance of the contributions by others.

Q29: Work isn't fun.

- ☐ If you answered true, that sucks. You spend 1/3 of your life working. It's okay to enjoy what you do. One metric to measure the health of an organization is laughter. If you answered true, you may want to examine the health of your team. If you aren't having at least some fun at work, your team might be in the same spot.
- ☐ If you answered false, good for you. Just watch out for the people who believe you shouldn't have fun at work. They

confuse frowning with working hard. If they see you smiling, they might think you aren't working.

Q30: The big picture is important.

- ☐ A true answer indicates that you are focusing on strategic issues; however, sometimes big-picture thinkers fail to define the details. Make sure that you aren't missing the trees in the forest.
- ☐ A false answer might indicate that you aren't being sufficiently strategic. Watch out for firefighting mode and lack of strategic vision.

Q31: Change is important.

- ☐ If you answered yes, you recognize the importance of change in an organization; however, you might be seen as changing for the sake of change. Make sure you understand the organizational change climate, your organization's tolerance for change, and that you invest in change management. Most organizational changes fail due to a lack of change management and misunderstanding the process required for change.
- ☐ If you answered false, you might be one of the people who say, "that's the way we've always done it." People hate those people. Try to be open to change. Watch out for shutting down people who want to try new things.

Q32: Maintaining the status quo is important.

This is the other side of the coin of Q31.

- ☐ A true answer recognizes that organizations cannot be in a constant state of change. There needs to be continuity. We need to focus on executing the process, but make sure that we continually evolve. Make sure that you listen to and support change initiatives.

- ☐ If you answered false, you might like to change a little too much. Your organization has core business value propositions and core behaviors that are part of its DNA that are valuable. Make sure that you recognize and value that DNA.

Q33: I'm too busy to plan.

- ☐ Firefighters' syndrome is where the excitement of dealing with urgency becomes a reinforcer for dealing with urgent problems only. Focusing on the immediate issues may result in a lack of strategic focus and lack of proactive thought leadership
- ☐ If one fails to address immediate problems, some might see this as a lack of action or an inability to address the immediate needs of the business.

Q34: I wish my employees would do what I said.

- ☐ If you answered true, you might undervalue the importance of autonomy. Autonomy means that people want some control over what they do. Make sure that you aren't micromanaging your people. Make sure that you listen and incorporate the feedback of others into your direction. Give people latitude in how they do a job.
- ☐ If you answered false, you may want to think about the importance of providing direction. Employees want to understand the expectations of their boss. They generally want to do a good job and meet the expectations of their boss.

Q35: People understand me.

- ☐ Wiio's law states, "Communication generally fails except by accident." If you believe people understand you, you may false to repeat your communication. One way to help communication not fail is to repeat communication. If you answered true, you might fail to understand how difficult communication is. You might also fail to understand your role in communication.

- [ ] If you answered false, you may need to think about your communication habits. Do not underestimate the importance of communication. People have a tendency to avoid doing things they think cannot do. Make sure you aren't avoiding communication because you struggle to do it well.

Q36: I'm not charismatic.

- [ ] Many people overestimate the importance of charisma for effective leadership. Charisma is important is being recognized as a leader, but it isn't important in leadership effectiveness. Make sure that you aren't limiting your leadership potential through negative self-talk.
- [ ] If you answered false, you believe you are charismatic. This is fine but you should know that some people see charismatic leaders as "all show, no substance." Make sure your actions align with your words.

Q37: I hate giving negative feedback.

- [ ] Most leaders hate giving negative feedback. They avoid addressing problems that erode their ability to lead. Employees view leaders who don't address problems as weak and ineffective. If you answered true, make sure that you aren't avoiding dealing with the problems in your organization.
- [ ] If you answered false, you are stating that you don't hate giving negative feedback. This is fine... just don't make sure you *like* it. If you like giving negative feedback, you might be overly critical, nitpicking, or misunderstand your role in other peoples' failures.

Q38: My boss does not want my feedback.

- [ ] A true answer could indicate that you undervalue your own observations, or it could indicate that you fear your boss and are afraid to be honest with her or him. This is the other side of conflict-avoidance.

- A false answer indicates that you understand the importance of feedback. Just make sure that your feedback is respectful and constructive.

Q39: It's important that my team get along.

- A true answer could indicate a tendency to need to avoid conflict. It could indicate a failure to address performance problems on your team.
- A false answer could indicate the importance of teamwork and collaboration.

Q40: I drive results.

- Although leaders should drive results, if believe that you drive results, you might not motivate and empower your team. If you answered true, be wary of a tendency to command and control.
- If you answered false, make sure that you are delivering results. Leaders must create results or eventually, they will not lead.

Q41: Sometimes a leader should just make a decision.

- A true answer might indicate that a lack of collaboration and a lack of seeking input from others.
- A false answer might be a warning sign that you need to be a bit more decisive.

Q42: Leaders deserve trust.

- If you answered true, you might have forgotten that trust is earned. A title does not guarantee trust. Trust is something that you earn every day and can lose in an instant.
- If you answered false, examine whether or not you have a trust issue with

Q43: Leaders need to be experts in their area.

- When people are promoted because of expertise, they often retain the need to continue to be an expert. An answer of true means could mean that you've fallen into the "leader as expert" trap. Leaders who fall into this trap make miss the other tools that a leader can use to lead.
- A false answer might indicate a failure to recognize the importance of expert power for effective leadership.

Q44: People need to have a say in what they do.

Giving people autonomy is an important piece of employee engagement and motivation; however, like anything else, one can take this too far.

- If you answered true, ask yourself if you are providing adequate direction and guidance. Don't fall into the habit of leading by consensus.
- If you answered false, you may want to examine your attitude toward employee autonomy. If you don't give people some latitude in their job responsibilities, you are less likely to have their full commitment.

Q45: Listening to others' opinions is important.

Most managers will acknowledge that they listen to the opinions of others; however, like all other attitudes, this can be taken too far.

- A true answer might indicate leading by consensus or poll taking. You might be seen as indecisive. Make sure that you aren't letting others' opinions keep you from making the decisions your organization and team need.
- If you answered false, you may take pride in your decisiveness, but you might be missing opportunities to benefit from other's expertise. You also might be reducing engagement.

Q46: I like to have all the facts before deciding.

This is another Catch-22. I love making decisions based on data. I want to understand the facts, not someone's opinion. But one can take this too far also.

- [ ] If you answered true, you might be accused of analysis paralysis. You might delay decisions until you have more data and you might be seen as indecisive.
- [ ] If you answered false, you might be seen as shooting from the hip. Frequent, rapid new decisions (direction) can also be seen as indecisiveness. Rock meet hard place.

Q47: Employees want to be left alone to do their job.

- [ ] Constant well-intentioned managerial involvement can be disruptive to productivity. A true answer recognizes that disruption; however, it could demonstrate a lack of communication, direction, or connection with your employees.
- [ ] A false answer might neglect the need to give your team the time to actually do the work.

Q48: I don't like to ask for help.

- [ ] If you answered true, you may be missing an opportunity to grow people through delegation. You also might be failing to collaborate.
- [ ] If you answered false, make sure that your effects to include people don't disrupt their responsibilities and reduce short-term productivity needs.

Q49: My team has everything they need to do their job.

This question deserves a fair amount of thought regardless of your answer.

- [ ] If you answered true, is this your opinion or does your team think they have everything they need? Are you properly vetting your resource needs? Managers need to be fiscally responsible.

Make sure that you have been adequately vetting your resourcing decisions so that you aren't perceived as irresponsible.

☐ If you answered false, you might want to think about the cost of not spending money. Yes, not spending the right money costs something. It reduces productivity. It reduces morale. It reduces the ability to innovate. You don't need to buy everything but you do need to buy the right things.

Q50: Training should be relevant to the current job.

Training provides an opportunity to grow your employees and yourself. When training opportunities come up, managers need to vet which training is appropriate and which training may not right for the organization. Your attitude about training might reveal something about you.

☐ If you answered true, you might undervalue the importance of training for strategic thinking. You might only train people for the immediate needs of your company. You may not be thinking about the future strategic direction of your organization. You might miss opportunities to improve.

☐ If you answered false, you may not be vetting your training budget adequately. You might need to focus on tactical performance.

Q51: You should celebrate team wins.

Acknowledging your team's successes recognizes the effort that they put into achieving a goal and reinforces the importance of their work.

☐ If you answered true, you recognize the importance of recognizing their work. Just make sure that you don't only pay attention to the results. Sometimes a team will extend effort and still fail. It's worth acknowledging effort even if it wasn't successful.

- [ ] If you answered false, you may want to think about why you feel you shouldn't celebrate success. Your employees thrive based on feedback. Acknowledging their efforts is an important way to motivate your team.

Q52: Celebrating individuals might create rivalry.

I've had people say to me, "If I single out one person, others will think that I'm showing favorites or 'why didn't he acknowledge me'."

- If you answered true, you might be afraid your people will think this and not celebrate individual successes.
- If you answered false, you need to remember the importance of acknowledging group wins.

A lot of this chapter might seem repetitive. I wanted you to examine your attitudes and beliefs. As we discussed earlier, attitudes may not be rational. I asked you to answer honestly. Remember that attitudes influence the other three As. It was important to spend a fair amount of time digging at your attitudes.

As you went through these 53 questions, I asked you to mark anything that *could* be true. I said that even if something *could* be true for you or if anyone has *ever* said this to you (even if you don't believe it), mark it.

There is a fair amount of overlap in these attitudes. Patterns are important. Review your checkmarks and mark anything that repeats. Take the top five and add those to your UNF*CK LEADERSHIP! Character Sheet.

CHAPTER 10: THE RULES OF THE GAME

"At one time it was winning awards, selling out concert dates, selling more albums than anyone else. Now, my goals are to see my grandchildren grown, live a long and healthy life with my family and friends and travel the world." – Reba McEntire

The last attitude we talked about asked about how a leader wins. Speaking of winning as a leader, I have a story about winning. (Of course, you do, Rettig. You have stories about everything.)

My wife, daughter, and I like to play board games. We have an entire bookshelf of games in our front room. Really.

Ignore the bottles of tequila on top.

One day we were playing a new game: Smallworld, a strategic game that feels like a high-fantasy version of Risk. I'm crazy competitive and (for better or worse) my daughter has inherited that trait. After my wife kicked both of our butts (by no small margin), my daughter looked frazzled. Since Smallworld is new to us, I wondered if she didn't like the game, so I asked, "Not a great game?"

She said, "No, it's fun. I just hate losing."

Now no one likes losing but something about her comment stuck with me. I had lost, but I enjoyed myself. In fact, I didn't really care if I won or lost the game. I felt like I had lost some essential part of myself: Competitive David was dead. But that wasn't true. I still strive to be the best in everything I do. I got a second master's degree because I wanted to differentiate myself from every other MBA. I'm back in school again because I want to be the best leader I can and help develop more great leaders. I wrote this book to develop great leaders.

That's when the light went on. I didn't care about winning Smallworld because *I wasn't playing to win the game*. I was playing to spend time with my 18-year old daughter and my wife. If winning means accomplishing your goal, I did win. I spent time with my daughter and wife. I should have been studying or writing or growing my consulting business, but I wanted to give them my time to show them they are valuable. I had redefined how I win.

Many new leaders fail to adjust to their new responsibilities. People sometimes get promoted because they are competent in a role, perhaps the best salesperson or the best engineer. They assume that the technical knowledge (engineer) or perseverance (salesperson), which got them promoted, will serve them in their leader role. This assumption is wrong and leads to failure as a leader.

WINNING AS AN IT GEEK

My first book was UNF*CK IT! I wrote about my time as an IT contributor and IT leader.

When I was in the day-to-day IT operations, I defined winning as being the best technical person I could. I chased the best, highest certifications from Microsoft, Cisco, Red Hat, CompTIA, ITIL, and a ton of others. The breadth and depth of my technical skills enabled me to approach problems from a variety of angles and I ended up bridging the gap between software developers, server admins, networking gurus, and database guys when all the finger-pointing started.

I didn't care whose fault it was; I wanted to solve the problem. These technical skills eventually gave me my first manager job.

WINNING AS A MANAGER

After my promotion, I no longer focused on being the best technical person. As a manager, I wanted the best team. I had redefined winning as a manager. For me, winning now meant that my team was the most productive, most helpful, had the best KPIs, and had the best reputation. I did whatever I could to expand my team's skills and push them for more and better performance.

WINNING AS A DIRECTOR

Eventually, this led to another promotion to a leader of leaders. As a director, I wanted my supervisors/managers to be the best leaders because great leaders produce great teams. Once again, I had redefined winning as "I win by helping my managers and supervisors be awesome."

WINNING AS A CONSULTANT AND AUTHOR

Now I see winning as helping my clients improve. If you hire me or read my book and get something out of it, I win. If I sell 1,000,000 books but no one becomes a better leader because of that, I lose. And I **hate** losing.

Why Leadership is like Roleplaying games

As I said, I was a Dungeons & Dragons geek. Loved it. Played at school, after school, and when I wasn't playing, I would read the rulebooks and create new characters. One of the interesting things about Dungeons & Dragons is how you win. If you haven't played a roleplaying game, let me tell you, in general, how you win.

You don't. Not in the traditional sense. Most games have a goal: accumulate the most points, money, tokens, chips, or whatever; get rid of all your cards or something, or collect a specific set of something. When you achieve the goal, the game is over. There are winners and losers. But not roleplaying.

Roleplaying **does** have short-term goals. Explore the dungeon. Kill the monster. Save the Princess. Kill the six-fingered man. But completing that short-term goal doesn't end the game. In roleplaying games, after you complete the short-term goal, you "level-up". Leveling-up makes you a little better at something (casting magic spells, shooting your six-shooter, wielding a light-saber). And being a little better at something allows you to take on the next short-term goal better. And the game goes on...

That's like leadership.

Leaders win by being better leaders.

To lead effectively, **you must redefine winning**. You need to be the best at helping your team be the best. And you help your team be the best by becoming the best version of you. If that doesn't sound interesting to you, you should really think about your career direction.

Another way leadership is like roleplaying, there's no one right way to do a roleplaying character. In fantasy roleplaying games, two common archetypes are The Warrior and The Magician. Let's compare them:

The Warrior	The Magician
• Physically strong • May wear heavy armor • Wields big weapons	• Intelligent • Casts magical spells • Uses magic scrolls, wands, etc.

Which is better, The Warrior or The Magician? There are a lot of opinions about which one is better, but it's likely a matter of personal preferences and doing what you enjoy. Ask that question at your local roleplaying convention and let the geek rage commence! In a balanced game, The Warrior and The Magician should be equivalent. You can play a warrior or magician and can level-up either. There's no right answer.

Leadership is a lot like that too. It doesn't matter whether you follow Bass's Transformational Leadership theory or Hersey & Blanchard's Situational Leadership Theory or Evans & Houses Path-Goal Leadership Theory. All of them are valid theories (although there are a lot of personal opinions). Ask which one is better at your local academic convention and let the academic rage commence!

Some leadership practices align better with some cultures, but in general, as long as you – as a leader – are leveling-up, you are winning.

CHAPTER 11: NOW WHAT?

"A word of advice is, when you judge someone, it doesn't define the person that you're judging. It defines you." – Tulisa

You've completed an UNF*CK LEADERSHIP character sheet. This is your personal leadership profile of yourself. It provides an overview of your aptitudes, attitudes, actions, and abilities. This gives you a starting point.

UNF*CK LEADERSHIP!
Character Sheet

Name: _____

Role: _____

Leadership Level (B-K Score): _____

Feedback Modifier (-10 to +10): _____

Aptitudes	Abilities
(1) _____	(1) _____
(2) _____	(2) _____
(3) _____	(3) _____
(4) _____	(4) _____
(5) _____	(5) _____

Other abilities _____

_____

_____

Self-assessment and reflection are foundational pieces of leadership development. A smart person (clearly, you... as a reader of my book, I assume you are bright, intelligent, and good-looking...) might note that these character sheet results are completely subjective. Yup.

A lot of leadership development programs include some type of assessment, but the assessments are often based on some subjective, pseudo-scientific tests. Some of these pseudo-scientific tests have become widely adopted; however, the scientific validity of these tests is spurious. One test, let's call it BlunderDick, was designed by a student (not a doctor) and measures general intelligence, but general intelligence is not an adequate predictor of performance. Another popular test, let's call it Liars-Bigs. Liars-Bigs attempts to classify people into one of sixteen groups which is exactly four more than a horoscope, which makes it 133% times as accurate as a horoscope. (For the math-challenged, horoscopes are 0% accurate... 0% multiplied by 133% is...)

However, we love self-assessment tests. Online and print personality tests are everywhere. They validate our awesomeness, our uniqueness, and our general amazingness... to ourselves. In fact, some people compare their scores with others.

Some people really like to brag about their BlunderDick score or their Liars-Bigs profile or their IQ. I'd like to quote the late-great Stephen Hawking, who said, "People who boast about their IQ are losers."

I'll show you my IQ score if you show me yours. And, if you're curious about my Liars-Bigs, I'm an AHOL.

HR departments really like these two tests even though there is very, very, very, very, very, very, very little evidence that they predict one damn thing and that gaming the tests are rampant. Why are these tests so popular? A great marketing department by the companies that sell the tests. A large chunk of the research supporting these tests is sponsored by the testing company. Marketing.

You might ask, "If I'm so down on these tests, why did you just have me fill that sheet out?" I'm not down on <u>assessment</u>. I am down on using assessment to judge who you are. You are more than a number or four-letters.

I'll tell you another story. I went to a new doctor. The nurse comes in, weighs me, pokes me, prods me, writes down a bunch of notes, and I sit and wait. After far-too-long, the doc sticks his head in the door, looks at me, and then looks at his chart. He looks at the number on the door, looks at the clipboard again, looks at me, and asks, "Mr. Rettig?"

"Yup."

"I'm sorry. I was just shocked. With your blood pressure, heart rate, blood tests, I was expecting a young athlete. Your numbers are amazing. I would tell you to lose weight... but there's really no reason."

I get on the scale every morning. Today, I weigh 329 pounds. Maybe 330 after I finish this box of Pop-tarts. What does that tell you about me? Nothing at all. Does it mean I'm lazy? I hope not. I run a consulting company, speak nationally, and am a full-time student. Unathletic? I have a black belt in Iron Tiger Kung Fu. Unhealthy? The doc doesn't think so. A good worker? A bad worker? A bad human? No. IQ, weight, skin color, gender, eye color, height, race, age... they are all just categories that we like to put people in so that we don't have to think about them as individuals.

The breakfast of authors...

Would you want people to judge you on a number?

Stop it.

Use your brain to learn about people as unique, amazing individuals. Stop relying on useless tests to screen employees or people.

End of rant.

So why did you complete the sheet? To give you a starting point, so you can plan how you want to level-up. Before you start leveling-up, you might want to understand the expectations for you as a leader. To do that, you need a framework for understanding your organizational situation.

CHAPTER 12: THE SITUATION

"If you can't put yourself in a situation where you are uncomfortable, then you will never grow." – Jason Reynolds

Do you act the same way in every situation? Before you answer, imagine yourself at a sporting event. Maybe watching the big game at your house filled with friends, food, and fun. How would you act? Cheering? Smiling? Loud? What if instead of the big game, what if it was a wake (or reception after a funeral)? Still your house... still lots of food... cheering? Probably not. Smiling? Nope. Loud? Doubtful.

We behave differently in different situations. Everyone does. It's expected and normal.

Does every manager come into the same situation? Absolutely not. Four common situations a manager can come into a turn-up, turn-around, tune-up, and transitioning. These four situations can be placed on a graph where X shows alignment with the business values and Y shows the performance.

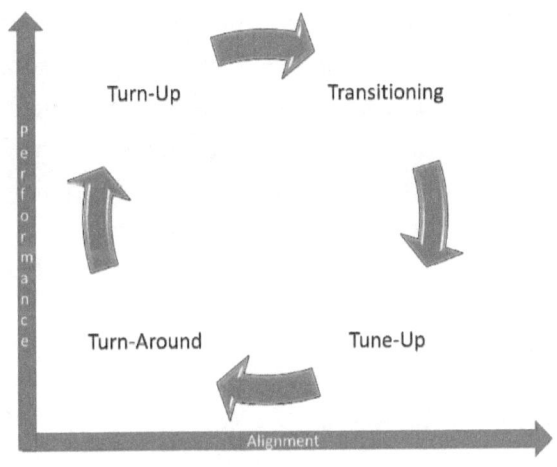

TURN-UP

Turn-up situations are companies that are just starting or undergoing rapid growth. This is represented by the up arrow. As a leader, you will be expected to hire the right people to support the new or growing business. You will be expected to establish the right processes and procedures that will grow with the organization. You will need to understand the business competencies to align your departmental activities with the value proposition of the business. Your priorities are **hiring, defining and aligning.**

PRIORITIES

- **Hiring** the right people
- **Defining** the processes
- **Defining** the procedures
- **Defining** the organizational value proposition
- **Aligning** with the organizational value proposition

TRANSITIONING

A transitioning situation is where an established department or business is changing leaders but not facing major organizational challenges. This is represented by the top right-facing arrow. Things are moving in the right direction and are "on-top" of their game. There are no major initiatives, no performance issues, and no alignment problems. A leader coming into this situation needs to spend time learning about the people, processes, and procedures while maintaining the current performance. At the same time, the leader needs to look for areas of opportunity, but make changes slowly so they don't disturb the existing performance. Your priorities are **learning and looking**.

PRIORITIES

- **Learning** about people
- **Learning** about the processes
- **Learning** about the procedures

- **Learning** the organizational/department value proposition
- **Looking** for opportunities to slowly make a difference.

TUNE-UP

Tune-up situations are where department or organization are aligned with the organizational value proposition, but not performing at the level that they need. The downward pointing arrow indicates the downward performance trends. I tend to spend most of my consulting time in tune-up and turnaround situations (like 80% of my time). The department is doing the right things, but not delivering at the speed or value to meet expectations. A leader coming into this situation needs to spend time learning about the people, processes, and procedures while rapidly identifying areas of opportunity to make a difference. Your priorities are **assessing and accelerating.**

PRIORITIES
- **Assessing** the people
- **Assessing** the processes
- **Assessing** the procedures
- **Assessing** the value proposition
- **Accelerating** results.

TURN-AROUND

Turn-around situations are represented by the bottom arrow. The department, team, or organization is going the wrong direction and they are not performing at the needed or expected level. My book UNF*CK IT! presents my framework for turning around IT departments, but the framework in UNF*CK IT can be applied to any turn-around situation. My career was built on turning-around underperforming teams. I still spend a lot of time consulting in these situations. A leader in this situation is expected to change the team direction and change the performance level. This is often harder than any of the other three situations because of the entrenched people, processes, and procedures that have created a system of a culture of poor performance. I can't rewrite all of UNF*CK IT! in a paragraph, but a leader in this situation should **realign, remove, and refocus.**

Priorities

- **Realign** the people
- **Realign** the processes
- **Realign** the procedures
- **Remove** any people that do not deliver business value.
- **Remove** any processes that do not deliver business value.
- **Remove** any procedures that do not deliver business value.
- **Refocus** the freed-up resources (from the removal) to people, processes, and procedures that deliver business value.

Throughout this chapter, I talked about business value. Business value has a very specific definition, that's important to understand. Let's define business value and how to determine your business value. If you read UNF*CK IT!, this is the same framework presented there, but without the IT-specific bits. If you want more detail on alignment, I'd recommend that book. The author is amazing and he needs the money...

CHAPTER 13: WHAT WOULD YOU SAY YOU DO HERE

"If you ask me, 'So what is your business model?' Our business model's always about shifting to higher-value opportunities." – Ginni Rometty

We talked a lot about value in this section. It's important when you read "value", you know exactly what I mean. I've spent a lot of time in lean manufacturing environments and I like the Kaizen definition of value: **value is anything that your customer will pay for.**

> Value [/'valy$\overline{oo}$/]
>
> *Noun*
>
> 1. Anything your customer will pay for.
> 2. That's it. Sorry, buddy.

Some people like to argue that if it is important, it's valuable. I don't see it that way. Only one person determines value: the people who buy and pay for the company's products: whether that's pampoogas, pantookas, or drums!

If the company's customer would buy more pantookas through an iPhone application, then an iPhone application adds **value**. If an iPhone app is nifty and everybody in the company thinks we need to do it, but the customer doesn't give a rat's ass, the iPhone app does not add value. Period.

I'm not saying that businesses will only do things that customers will pay for. Absolutely not. Do you think the customer gives one rats' ass about whether or not you have a copier in HR? Or an executive assistant? Or plants in the office? **I am saying if we need to align your**

department with your business's CVP as much as possible to deliver value. Are we on the same page again? Good.

Now, you might disagree with that definition of value and you are *allowed to disagree.* But for the framework presented in this book, we are going to use this definition. If you define value differently and try to apply the concepts in this book, you're going to be disappointed.

I'm saying that when I talk about value, I specifically mean "anything the company's customer will pay for".

To assess a business's value, you need to understand why your customers buy your stuff. Whether your stuff is a thing, a service, or an idea, you have customers and they buy your stuff.

- If you make soap (a thing), your customers buy your soap because it has "something" that they want more than another soap. They give you money to have that "something"
- If you wash dogs (a service), your customers choose you to wash their dog because you have "something" that they want more than another dog washer. It could be a relationship with the dog, a friendly smile, or you are the closest... but it is "something". They give you money for that something.
- If you run a nonprofit charity that raises money for saving the Kitti's hog-nosed bat (an idea), your donors and volunteers are your customers (they give you something of value: money or time) for "something" that your charity does. It could be a shared belief about how cute Kitti's hog-nosed bat is, it could be community service to avoid jail, it could be part of a corporate social responsibility initiative and part of their "we are not an evil empire" media campaign. The point is: you provide something that they value in exchange for something you value.

Seriously, look how cute it is.

These "somethings" are how your business generates value or your Customer-Value-Proposition (CVP).

Your business can generate value through a variety of Customer-Value-Propositions (CVP), such as features/benefits/attributes, price, availability/exclusivity, quality, brand awareness/reputation, variety, service, relationship, convenience, customization/personalization, or association with another value (such as environmental products or products designed to appeal to a specific race, nationality, religious group).

Knowing how your business's Customer-Value-Proposition (CVP) is very important for this book. Actually, it's critically important for running a business.

Competitors in the same business have different CVPs. For example, let's create three imaginary coffee shops.

Five-Pointed-Deer is a nationally-recognized, trendy coffee shop that sells coffee and a variety of sugary desserts disguised as coffee drinks. The customers come there because they have good coffee (features), they are everywhere (availability), they are consistent (quality), they advertise the fuck out of themselves (brand awareness), the service is good (duh - service), and they make every sugary drink under the sun (variety) and if they don't they'll mix up whatever concoction you can imagine.

Your-Neighborhood-Coffee-Shop is a local, small-town coffee shop that tries to position itself as the anti-Five-Pointed-Deer. The customers come there because they have coffee from a local roaster (features), they learn all the regulars' names and drink preferences (relationships), and association with their small town by supporting other small-town events.

I-Guess-This-Is-Coffee is a coffee shop started by a couple of retired buddies as a place to get together and hang out. They didn't want a bunch of kids or that-crap-kids-are-calling-music-now-a-days playing. They wanted someplace to shoot the shit with their friends and get a cup of joe. Some other retirees started coming and it's become the place-to-be for the local silver-haired people. The coffee is whatever's-cheapest-at-the-grocery-this-week, run through a drip coffee maker that looks older than the two guys running the place, and served in some cheap-ass Styrofoam cups. Get it yourself and put a buck in the jar. People come there for the price (cheap), the relationships (everybody knows everybody), and the association with retirees.

All three fictional places sell coffee but understanding their CVPs makes a world of difference in how the coffee shops market and how they operate.

Take a few minutes to fill this out:

My business creates value for our customers by: _____

_____

_____

_____

The next step is to figure out how you do the things that create the value. What are you good at that enables your company to provide great service or make the highest quality thing-a-mabobs or establish exclusive partnerships with the Alien Overlords of Planet X... however you defined value before. The things that you do that create value are your business's competencies or Value-Supporting-Competencies (VSC). Value-Supporting-Competencies (VSC) are the engines that produce value.

Let's revisit one of the fictional coffee shops:

Five-Pointed-Deer value propositions:

- Good coffee (features)
- Located everywhere (availability)
- Consistent (quality)
- Advertise the fuck out of themselves (brand awareness)
- Good service
- Lots of different sugary drinks
- Customized sugary drinks

To determine the Value-Supporting-Competencies (VSC) that enable creating value, Five-Pointed-Deer must ask, "How do we do _____?" for each value-proposition.

- **How does Five-Pointed-Deer get good coffee?** They use their size to negotiate exclusive supplier agreements with the best bean suppliers. They taste test everything. They only ship the best beans to their ubiquitous caffeine & sugar crack houses.
- **How does Five-Pointed-Deer establish locations everywhere?** Profitable growth and reinvesting cash in new store acquisition.
- **How does Five-Pointed-Deer ensure consistency?** They taste test everything. They only ship the best beans to their coffee shops.
- **How does Five-Pointed-Deer create brand awareness?** Dedicated budget to advertising and social media presence.

- **How does Five-Pointed-Deer provide good service?**
  Standardized extensive corporate training upon being hired and every six-months. Customer service is reinforced in every meeting and message from the home office. And the shock collars hidden in the workers' uniforms.
- **How does Five-Pointed-Deer have so many different sugary drinks?** All custom orders from all locations are sent back to the corporate office. For repeated orders for the same custom drink, a test kitchen reproduces the recipe. We test consumer response and if it's positive, we add it to the menu, usually as a limited-time drink.
- **How does Five-Pointed-Deer customize sugary drinks?** By maintaining a large variety of flavored sugar goop to pour in coffee and making customers aware that they can have it however they like.

Based on that analysis, we could say Five-Pointed-Deer's competencies are:

- Exclusive supplier agreements with bean suppliers
- Taste-testing facilities
- Reinvesting profits in new store acquisition
- Advertising and social media
- Corporate training and retraining (and shock collars)
- Analyzing store sales to identify new concoctions
- Keeping stores stocked with lots of flavors

Let's do one more just to make sure we've got it.

Your-Neighborhood-Coffee-Shop value propositions:

- Coffee from a local roaster
- Learn all the regulars' names and drink preferences
- Association with their small town by supporting other small-town events.

Now, let's figure out their Value-Supporting-Competencies (VSC):

- **How does Your-Neighborhood-Coffee-Shop get coffee from a local roaster?** They found a local roaster online and visited them. They talked to the local roaster about the challenges of being a local business and offered to work together.
- **How does Your-Neighborhood-Coffee-Shop learn all the regulars' names?** They tell employees to ask the customers' names and use them three times when they first meet. They put the customers' names with the order into their computers. They have weekly contests with decent prizes for the employee who gets the most names right and orders right.
- **How does Your-Neighborhood-Coffee-Shop connect with their small town and support local events?** They monitor the local paper. If any new events appear, they visit the event coordinator and talk about the importance of supporting local events and local businesses and look for a way to work together.

Based on that analysis, we would say Your-Neighborhood-Coffee-Shop's VSC are:

- Connecting with local roasters
- Training employees on their values
- Connecting with local events.

Now, let's do your company. What does your company do to creates those values that customers pay for?

- How does your company do _____?

- How does your company do _____?

- How does your company do _____?

- How does your company do _____?

127

- How does your company do _____?

Now, turn that list into Value-Supporting-Competencies (VSC) (your company will probably have more than four):

1. _____

2. _____

3. _____

4. _____

Imagine you are the CEO of Five-Pointed-Deer Coffee. Remember, the things you do that make your company money (VSC) are:

- Exclusive supplier agreements with bean suppliers
- Taste-testing facilities
- Reinvesting profits in new store acquisition
- Advertising and social media
- Corporate training and retraining (and shock collars)
- Analyzing store sales to identify new concoctions
- Keeping stores stocked with lots of flavors

Imagine I work for you. Imagine Brad Pitt. Now think of the exact opposite of Brad Pitt. That's me.

I come to you and say, "I found a way to analyze the store sales to identify repeat orders and identify new concoctions."

Are you interested? **Of course.** This aligned exactly with your VSC of "Analyzing store sales to identify new concoctions"

What if I came to you and said, "I found a local coffee roaster and think we could offer their beans in one store."

Are you interested? **Nope.** This does not align with your VSC.

Imagine you are the owner of Your-Neighborhood-Coffee-Shop. Me again, working for you.

I say, "I can add a webcam to the cash registers so we can add our customers' pictures to their receipt with the customers' permission. We could use that to learn our customers' names and faces even better."

Interested? **Of course. It aligns with your VSC.**

Imagine instead I say, "I negotiated a deal with a global coffee roaster network which will let us offer exotic coffees from around the world!"

Interested? **Absolutely not.** The second your local roaster finds out that you are offering the same coffee like every other coffee shop in that network, you will lose all credibility with him and maybe everyone else. People will think you've gone corporate.

Once you understand your company's VSC, you can determine your alignment with these VSC.

VSC-Alignment Score is your department's total annual cost/the cost of activities that align with VSC.

Remember, **activities that don't align with VSC <u>can</u> be important, but they <u>do not deliver value.</u>**

Understanding your VSC Alignment will help determine If you are in a turn-up, turn-around, tune-up, and transitioning situation.

CHAPTER 14: GOOOOAAAAALLLLLLLLS!

"When it is obvious that the goals cannot be reached, don't adjust the goals, adjust the action steps." -- Confucius

After assessing yourself and your situation, we need to establish some goals for leveling-up your leadership. By understanding both yourself and your environment, you are in a great situation to create a plan to move forward.

Let's start with a quick mental exercise.

Who was the best leader you ever had? What was their name?

_____ was the best leader I ever had.

Think about the best leader you ever had. Someone you really admire. Someone who you want to be like. How did they make you feel about coming to work? How did they make you feel about yourself? Spend a few minutes soaking in that feeling. If you like to write, write something about them. If you have maintained contact with them, call them and tell them what a difference they made.

I can tell you that leaders thrive on that kind of feedback. Leadership is the hardest job you'll ever do. A great leader takes none of the credit and all of the blame and sometimes it's soul-crushing. It feels <u>great</u> to have someone tell you that they appreciate your leadership. Whenever I'm feeling the pressures of leadership or questioning my decisions, I read some of the quotes from my LinkedIn profile: "Without hesitation, David is the best boss I have ever had in nearly every way", "David is one of those leaders who has a way of bringing the best out of his people", "...I can honestly say that he is the best boss I have ever had", etc... This feedback refuels me when the rest of my professional life is in the toilet. Stop now. Make a call. Send a note. Write something nice on LinkedIn to the best leader you ever had.

When you think about the best leader you ever had, what did they do that made them great? Write down one action.

A great leader does _____. (Action)

What did characteristics do they have that you admire? Write down one aptitude.

A great leader is _____. (Aptitude)

What skills did they have that you would like to have?

A great leader knows _____. (Ability)

Lastly, what do you think they believed about you?

A great leader believes _____. (Attitude)

You now have a list of goals for leveling-up your leadership.

1. _____ (Action)
2. _____ (Aptitude)
3. _____ (Ability)
4. _____ (Attitude)

Pick one or two from the list of four that you want to work on first. Which two of these goals align most with your organizational situation? Which would enable you to deliver value to the organization in the best possible way? Select those two.

Limit yourself to two level-up goals, because change is hard, because people over-estimate the amount of change they can accomplish in the short-term, and because it's better to accomplish one thing well than do a half-assed job on four things.

There's no right or wrong on which level-up goals that you want to improve.

Action items are short-term goals that you will do to support your level-up goals. Think of action items as "the next thing that I will do". You don't need to have a fully-mapped out long-term plan. Don't let lack of a comprehensive plan stop you from getting started. Action items should be feasible, useful, connected to your level-up goal, and goal you can keep because you are committed. I know this isn't as nearly as a memorable set of rules as something like SMART goals, but I'm certain we can find a clever mnemonic to help you remember it.

- Feasible
- Useful
- Connected to your level-up goal
- Keepable

FEASIBLE

While silver-bullet leadership books might encourage you to imagine some ideal self, your UNF*CK action item should be practical. No moonshot goals. No "I'm going to change everything about me." We are focusing on continual improvement. Change is difficult and if you set an overly ambitious goal, you could get discouraged and quit before you make any progress. Change is a process. Trust the process.

USEFUL

Useful action items are action items that will have an immediate effect on your level-up goals. For example, if your level-up goal is to mentor people, you might think, "I'll make a list of people that I should mentor" or "I'll listen to a mentoring podcast". Both of these are great ideas; however, neither will have an immediate effect on your level-up goals. You need something that will make an immediately visible difference.

CONNECTED

Action items should be connected to your level-up goals. Make sure that you pick an action-item that connects to one of your two level-up goals. Again, it's easy to find activities that don't have any effect on your level-up goals but to make a difference you need to connect the dots between your level-up goals and your action items.

KEEPABLE

Lastly, find action items that you are really committed to keeping. People come up with crazy action items in support of goals. For example, let's say you have a level-up goal of talking face-to-face with your employees. So you think, "I'm going to take one of my team out to lunch every day." Great action item. It's pure bullshit, but great action item. Something is going to come up. You know it is. And you're going to miss a day. And you're going to feel shitty about missing it. And then it's all over. The same thing happens all the time with dieters and exercisers. "I'm going to walk 2-miles every day." Bullshit. You're going to walk in a downpour? Nope. Instead, set action items that are so ridiculously easy that you will keep it.

For example, if you have a level-up goal of talking face-to-face with your employees, say, "I will talk to one employee for 5 minutes once a week." Wow. That's crazy easy. Yup. You can do that right now. If you have a level-up goal of giving praise, say, "I will say thank-you to one employee once a week." That's it. Tiny. Little. Baby. Steps.

When you have Feasible, Useful, Connected, and Keepable action-items, you start evolving into a better leader. You start leveling-up.

KEEPING THE GOALS IN FRONT OF YOU

Next, I want you to remind yourself of those goals every day by putting them in writing, in front of you, in locations where you will see them a few times a day. Write those down on three separate sheets of paper as positive, declaratory statements. For example,

"I will mentor people."

"I will be honest with people."

Stick one note on your bathroom mirror where you can read it every morning. Stick one note someplace on your desk where it is visible. Stick one note someplace else highly visible.

I would also suggest changing your logon password to remind yourself of your two goals. How many times a day do you have to type in a password? Every time you type "Password1", your brain recites it. Let's put that recitation to good use.

In the example above, I might use the password "MentorPeople&BeHonest1". Look at that awesome password! Upper-case letters, lower-case letters, a special symbol, a number, and 22 characters... your IT guy would be so proud. Howsecureismypassword.net says this password will take 252,000,000,000,000,000,000,000 years to crack (yet IT will make me change it in 90 days...).

Every time you need to type in that password, your brain will recite the mantra "Mentor People and Be Honest...one".

Last reminder... find an accountability partner. What's an accountability partner? Let's start with what an accountability partner is not. An accountability partner is not a nag. For example, if I wanted to stop eating Pop-tarts (over my cold dead body), I would not ask some kale eating, health nut. I would find a fellow Poptartoholic who also desired to stop eating the warm deliciousness given to us by God and we would help each other. An accountability partner should also want you to succeed, not look for you to fail.

You are unlikely to find someone with exactly the same goals as you. However, you can find someone with the same broad goals of leveling-up their leadership. The easiest way would be to find someone else with a copy of this book.

Here's a script to ask them to be your accountability partner. Please read it word for word. Each word is critically important.

> "Dude! (or Dudette!) Great book! Have you gotten to the Level-Up chapter yet? You should post a 5-star review on Amazon. Listen, I need an accountability partner. Are you interested? We can start immediately after you post that 5-star review on Amazon."

If you read this script word-for-word, I guarantee that I will appreciate it. And you might find an accountability partner.

WHAT SHOULD AN ACCOUNTABILITY PARTNER DO?

Now that you've both posted a 5-star review and agreed to be accountability partners, what do you do?

1. Exchange contact information.
2. Exchange your goals.
3. Schedule a weekly or biweekly check-in.
4. Encourage each other.

This is what *encouragement* sounds like. I feel like I need to define that because it's so rare at work.

Encourage

En·cour·age | \ in-ˈkər-ij

1. To inspire with courage.

And inspire means "to spur on" or "to motivate".

Encouraging someone is literally to spur them on by giving them courage. Trying to change is scary. You might fail. If your accountability partner misses their goal, your job is not to critique, correct, offer advice, tear down, or make your partner feel bad. **Your job is to spur**

them on by giving them courage. You are a cheerleader. When a team fails to score, a cheerleader doesn't go, "You should try this play next time". They don't say, "Didn't you realize how important that goal was? Jeez, what were you thinking?" But they don't also say, "You did great!!!" They say, "We believe in you! We believe in you!"

Coaches critique, correct, and offer advice. Not you. You are a cheerleader. Grab those pom-poms.

An accountability partner check-in sounds like this:

> "Last week you told me you wanted to advance your goal of _____ by doing _____. How did that go?"

> If your partner did their weekly short-term goal, you say, "Good job! You are doing the work to become a better leader."

> If your partner did not achieve their weekly short-term goal, you say, "You can do it. I know you can. I believe in you."

Your accountability partner sets their own goal and they work to achieve their own goal. If they don't do their goal, that's on them. That's it. Not your problem. Not your fault. Your job is <u>not</u> to get them to <u>do</u> the goal. **Your only job is to encourage your partner, so they stick with it.** That's it. Encourage. Say it with me. Now write it down.

_____

My only job is to encourage my accountability partner.

After you encourage them on last week's goal, you say, "What do you want to want to work on next week to level-up your leadership?" Then you *encourage* them. "You can do that! I know you can. I believe in you." <u>You give them the courage to become a better leader</u>.

Then the tables turn, your partner asks you the same thing. You tell them what you are going to do. You set your goals. You report on your actions and progress.

Sometimes an accountability partner will forget their role. With absolutely good intentions, they might offer advice, critique, or correct. I strongly suggest a friendly, non-threatening code phrase to remind them that they are a cheerleader, not a coach. I like the phrase, "What the fuck, dude", but you may want something gentler. Try, "Cheerleader" or "Omi" (he wrote that song... "I think I found myself a cheerleader...").

Now, if your accountability partner says "Omi" to you, <u>stop talking</u>. Take a breath. Don't apologize. Don't explain. Don't justify. Then say, "Thank you. I'll do better. I meant to say that you can do it. I know you can. I believe in you." I don't care if you have a brilliant insight that would fix everything. You have <u>one job</u>. Turn back a page. Look at your handwriting. You have one job: **Your only job is to encourage your partner, so they stick with it.**

WASH, RINSE, REPEAT

How long does this continue? I don't know how long do you breathe? Can you say, "Well, that seems like enough oxygen? I think I'm done breathing forever." You breathe or you die. **Self-improvement is like oxygen for leadership.** You grow or you die.

You and your accountability partner will continue to meet and work on your stuff until you get that action-item down, then find another action-item, and repeat the steps... repeat... repeat... repeat...

Once a year, it's appropriate to dust off the character sheet and evaluate your 4As. I like to do this when I do my employees' reviews. Employee reviews are a great time to revisit the getting feedback conversation on p. 78. By reviewing yourself when you review them, you demonstrate that you are committed to self-improvement. Doing an annual review of the organizational situation is appropriate as well.

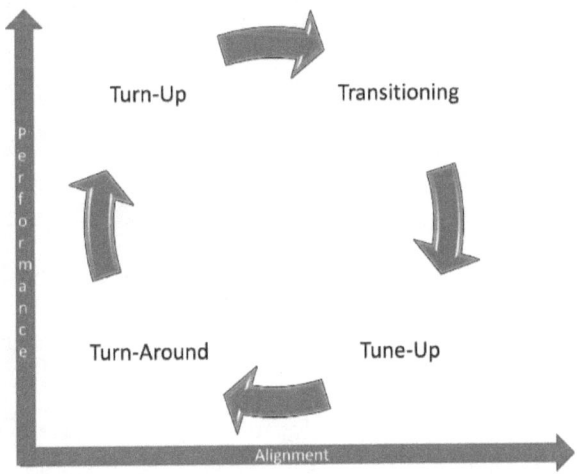

If you were in a **turn-up situation** and you have hired the right people, defined the right processes and procedures, and aligned with the Value-Supporting-Competencies, you've likely moved to a **transitioning situation** and need to shift focus to **looking** for new ways to improve performance.

If you were in a **transitioning situation** and looked for a way to improve performance, you might want to shift into a **tune-up mode**, assessing and accelerating the changes you identified.

If you were in a **tune-up** mode and accelerated the changes, you might be back in a **transitioning** situation and need to **look** for new ways to improve performance.

Lastly, if you were in a **turn-around situation** and you were able to get redirected and performing, you could move to a rapid growth **turn-up** situation or maybe you jump right to **transitioning**.

These annual periodic reviews of the situation ensure that you as a leader continue to drive value, improve performance, and are focusing on the right things.

SECTION 3 – LEADERSHIP COOKBOOK

CHAPTER 15: NO SECRET RECIPE

"If you're trying to create a company, it's like baking a cake. You have to have all the ingredients in the right proportion." – Elon Musk

By now, you should have sussed out that there is no secret recipe for leadership. You don't need to become me to be a great leader; you need to become the best version of you. It's a little like cooking. There is no one perfect cake; there are thousands of great cakes. You can tweak the recipe for the cake and maybe make it even better. You can change anything you want (as long as it has cream cheese frosting --- mmm cream cheese frosting...).

Leadership is the same way. I can't give you a recipe for becoming a great leader. But no one can. Anyone who tries is full of shit. Run far and fast from those books. You don't need to be Simon or Maxwell or Robbins. You need to be you. Just the best version of you.

However, I would feel remiss if I didn't offer you some tactical leadership guidance. But don't think of this as a recipe, think of these are ingredients. For example, I love salmon, but my wife hates it. If we had salmon as an ingredient, she might ignore that ingredient. I would add it.

Same for this. I'm going to list some of the ingredients that I use for leadership. If you think, "Man... I like that ingredient!", you have my permission to use it in your leadership recipe, but don't try to become me... be the best version of you.

Given that caveat, let me give you a few of my favorite ingredients. The following sections cover mentoring, dealing with conflict, setting expectations, modeling behaviors, dealing with micromanagement, delegating, influencing people, hiring, and interviewing. We will examine these ingredients from the 4As framework, so you can incorporate the ingredients you like into the 4As framework.

CHAPTER 16: FINDING A MENTOR

"The best piece of advice I've received is find a mentor, but also mentor others." – Eric Swalwell

Finding a mentor is an important ingredient for becoming a great leader. A mentor can provide feedback, help you overcome your biases, and help develop your attitude, aptitude, actions, and abilities.

A mentor is simply a more experienced individual who is willing to invest in you. A mentor does not need to be in the same profession or industry. In a purely selfish frame-of-reference, a mentor knows something that you don't know.

I've been fortunate to have an amazing set of mentors. No one told me that I needed a mentor. I established my mentoring relationships simply by dumb luck.

My first mentor, Greg, was my boss's boss at a $200M logistics company. I was the senior IT person; I had absolutely no interest in management.

I had built the company's email system and, as the company grew, the email system I built couldn't keep up. It started breaking nearly every week. I met with the owner of the business and explained all the technical problems and everything I had tried to fix the problem. Then I asked for $5,000 some bigger equipment to fix the issue. The owner replied, "David, you just don't understand the business."

I left his office distraught, head hung low, obviously wearing my failure and frustration on every inch of my body. My soon-to-be-mentor Greg saw my defeat and asked what was wrong. I recounted the story of my frustrated attempts to fix the broken email for the low price of $5,000.

Greg said, "Wait here", walked into the owner's office, and closed the door.

Five minutes later, he walked out and said, "I got you $50,000. Fix the email." My jaw dropped. Up was down. Black was white. Everything I knew was wrong. When my head stopped reeling, I said, "You know something I don't know. I need to know what you know."

Greg said, "Okay."

That was the moment Greg Schuth became my mentor.

It was dumb luck that changed my life.

Let's not make it dumb luck for you.

If your level-up goal is to find a mentor, let me give you some action items that you can use to help reach your level-up goals.

Think of someone who knows something that you don't know (ability), does something that you want to do (action), or believes something that you admire (attitude).

Contact that person.

In general, face-to-face is better than a phone call. A phone call is better than an email. Email is better than carrier pigeon (but only slightly). Scratch that. Use a carrier pigeon before email. Don't email someone to be a mentor.

The general conversation should go like this,

> "I've always admired how you _____. I'm looking for a mentor to help me learn to _____ (same as first blank). Would you be interested in being my mentor? If not, can you recommend someone who could help me learn to _____ (same as first and second blank)."

One of three things will happen.

1. They will say "no", and you can think of a different person.
2. They can say "yes". Woohoo! You have a mentor!
3. They can give you a different name.

If #1 or #3, take a different name and repeat the same cycle.

Don't take "no" personally. You don't know what they have going on. Maybe they are in the midst of a messy divorce. Maybe they are swamped with work right now. Maybe they are so insecure about their own leadership that they can't imagine having anything valuable to say. Maybe you are just too cute and if they were alone with you, they would leave their spouse and kids. A "no" is not about you; it's about them.

Regardless, eventually, you'll end up with a mentor who can help you level-up into the leader that you want to be. Now that you have a mentor what are you going to do with them?

SCHEDULING

Don't schedule mentoring meetings too frequently. Meeting too often will result in unproductive meetings or meetings that become more of an inconvenience rather than something you look forward to. I'd say once every two weeks is the absolute most often that you should meet. Once a month is likely better.

For your first meeting, learn about your mentor. Ask about their career, experience, and education. Listen. Answer their questions. Take notes, if that's not awkward. Try to find life-lessons from their experience that you can apply to your life. At the end of the meeting, thank them.

For your second meeting and all future meetings, you should thank them for the previous meeting. Share anything that you took away from the meeting, how you applied it to your life or career, and bring a topic for discussion. Appropriate topics might be, "I'm struggling with this decision. What would you do?" or "I want to learn this. How would you approach that?" or "Tell me what you think about this topic."

Remember, you are there to learn. To learn, you need to *listen* and *ask questions*. Not listen and tell them what you think. Not listen and then give your opinion. Not listen and argue. *Listen* and *ask questions*.

If your mentor asks you questions, answer them, but remember the point of a mentor is to teach you.

CHAPTER 17: LANCE THE BOIL

"Thought is an infection. In the case of certain thoughts, it becomes an epidemic." – Wallace Stevens

There's this super gross show on TV about this doctor who cuts open people and pulls nasty stuff out. I've never watched it. I have no desire to gag for 30 minutes. That is not entertaining for me. Some people love it. I avoid those people.

The idea is that people have an infection and this doctor removes the source of the infection so that they can heal. Sometimes they take a long sharp pokey-thing (a medical term) and poke the skin so that the nasty stuff comes out. That's called lancing the boil.

This happens with people too.

For example, I was managing a few teams in a large organization. The team was spread all over the world. Two of the leaders were in two different locations and they hated each other. For the sake of this story let's call them Cain and Abel. Cain and Abel hated each other. It might be a name thing.

At least once a week, Cain would call me and tell me what an idiot Abel was. Cain would tell me Abel did this wrong or that wrong and bitch and bitch and bitch.

At least once a week, Abel would call me and tell me how difficult it was to work with Cain. He wouldn't answer his emails. He was rude and condescending.

It was like listening to my kids arguing.

We had a leadership meeting where everyone flew in once a year, so I grabbed Cain and Abel and took them to a private room together. Three chairs. Nothing else.

I said, "Cain, you don't like Abel." Of course, Cain denied it. I continued, "Dude, you call me at least once a week telling me how Abel doesn't know how to do his job. And Abel, you don't like Cain. You call me at least once a week telling me how hard it is to work with Cain. Now talk."

Abel told Cain how he wanted to work with him but he felt like Cain dismissed everything he said. Abel said he would ask something to try to get more information, but Cain always made him feel stupid.

Cain talked about how Abel used to make snide remarks about him and say things about how Abel would exclude him from important meetings.

Abel said he excluded him because... and back and forth... further and further, until...

Abel said, "You know... when we first met five years ago, you offered to buy me a beer and I don't drink because of my religion. You made fun of me for not drinking."

Cain got red in the face. "Dude... I'm so sorry. I was being stupid and having fun and I just cracked a joke because I was uncomfortable."

Abel said, "I know but it hurt."

Cain apologized profusely and sincerely.

Five years of bickering and lost productivity because of one stupid ass comment.

What can we learn from this? The lesson isn't to watch everything you say, because that's stupid and impossible. You're going to piss someone off some time.

The lesson is: if we didn't get to the underlying problem, we'd be dealing with this stupidity for another 5 years.

You need to lance the boil.

YOU DON'T NEED A DOCTOR

You don't need to be the leader to lance the boil. There's someone in your organization that you hate working with. They grate your nerves. You avoid walking by their cubicle or office for fear that they are going to want to talk. You can lance that boil without someone else.

Let me tell you a story about someone lancing a boil with me.

I had just promoted a new supervisor. Unfortunately, the timing of the promotion was bad, and I was focused on other issues. She was out on her own for longer than she should have been. She called me and said, "You aren't giving me the leadership and direction I need."

Ouch. She was right. My reasons, the situation, didn't matter. I had a responsibility to her.

I said, "You're right. I'll be there next week." I flew in and spent the week with her giving her 100% of my time.

She could have let my lack of attention fester. It could have become a thing between us. Maybe it would have healed on its own, maybe not. But she wasn't a coward. She lanced the boil.

That's leadership.

ACTION ITEMS

If your level-up goal is to address conflict in your organization, you may want to lance the boil. This takes courage because ugly stuff sometimes comes out of that. Sometimes you only see a little red irritation on the surface and find out that underneath the skin is some seriously scary

151

gunk. Sometimes it's _easier_ to not lance the boil. Sometimes it's _easier_ to live with the infection.

But being a leader isn't about doing the easy thing. It's about doing the right thing.

Now if you want to live with the nasty infections in your team or organization, I want you to really think about what you are saying. You are saying, "I would rather live with an unhealthy team than do the hard work of cleaning this up." You might justify it with "I don't want to stir things up" or "I'm just smoothing things over" or "The team doesn't need conflict", but this is just dissembling. You really are choosing to live with a cancer that's eating your team's morale and productivity. If you see yourself as a peacekeeper (rather than a healer), I want you to look at yourself in the mirror and say, "I am choosing to not help my team." Does that feel good, Leader?

If you decide to deal with problems rather than hide from them, here's the steps for lancing the boil:

1. Get together with the other person.
2. Acknowledge the problem and your part in the problem.
3. Tell them that you want to make it better.
4. Talk _together_.

CARE AFTER TREATMENT

After you lance the boil, you have an open wound. The infection is gone, but open wounds need care, or the infection can return. That means regular meetings where you disinfect the wound with lots of communication and honesty. It's going to be sore for a while, but after a while, your organization will be all the healthier.

CHAPTER 18: MICROMANAGEMENT

"It's the people who are more insecure who feel the need to control and micromanage."– Sarah Gadon

At a team meeting, one of my teams talked about micromanagement. They all agreed micromanagement was bad and that they hated being micromanaged. I asked, "What is micromanagement?"

Everyone in the team could talk about times they felt had micromanaged, but found it challenging to nail down a clear definition. However, through the resulting conversation, we identified **some common actions that lead to feeling micromanaged** and the **attitudes that cause these actions.**

ACTIONS THAT CAUSE PEOPLE TO FEEL MICROMANAGED
Let's look at the actions that cause employees to feel micromanaged through the stories my team talked about.

NOT GIVING A "WHY"
One employee told a story about a manager telling him to do a task. He asked, "why?", not to challenge the manager. The employee thought there might be a better way to resolve the problem. The manager said, "You don't need to know why. Just do what I told you." The employee felt disrespected and devalued as a person.

MY WAY OR THE HIGHWAY
Another employee told another story about a manager telling him <u>how</u> to do a task. When the employee found another, more efficient way to complete the work, the manager became hostile and insisted he do the task the original way. The employee later found out the manager had created the original methodology. The employee felt

that the manager needed to be in control because they felt threatened by his abilities.

Do It Now
A different employee needed time to implement a solution. He told his boss that it would take him a week to "do it right." His boss told him that he needed it now and that he needed to do it faster. The employee felt like his boss did not trust him or his professional opinion.

Are We There Yet?
This employee's manager asked her for <u>daily</u> updates on a project that would take <u>months</u> and that did not change daily. When the employee asked about the frequency of the updates, her manager told her that she needed to continue the daily updates. The employee felt like her manager's boss didn't trust her manager and that the manager didn't have the strength of leadership to stand up for himself.

We see four actions that lead to the feeling that employees are being micromanaged: not giving an explanation, not giving autonomy on how to do the job, not listening to an employee regarding resource requirements, or checking up on employees or projects too often.

Micromanagers often think that high-pressure situations create feelings of micromanagement, but my research does not support this. Employees often said that **the most fun they ever had was in high-pressure situations**. High-pressure did not make them feel micromanaged because they felt confident to work hard and get things done. <u>However</u>, *an insecure manager* **is more likely to micromanage people during high-pressure situations**. They are more likely to be too rushed to give a "why", feel like they have to give specific directions, push people to go faster and faster, and demand frequent updates.

Mitigating Micromanagement
Let's look at the actions and attitudes that can mitigate feelings of micromanagement.

As a leader, you need to explain why your team is doing something. Explain "why" we need the solution, "why" the timeline, and "why" you are requesting updates. If you don't know you need to ask your boss or your boss's boss or the stakeholders. You need to ask "why" until you can explain why and own the explanation. "Because my boss told me to" is not a valid reason to give your team.

Start with why you are asking "why?"

As the victim of a micromanager, ask "why". The phrasing of your question is really important, as this might be the first time your boss has been asked. Start with why you are asking "why?"

Here are a few **examples of how to deal with micromanagers**. In each, I've underlined the "why".

- If you don't know why you are doing a project, ask, "<u>I want to better understand our business processes.</u> Can you tell me why this project supports the business?"

- If your boss tells you to do something a specific way, you can say, "<u>I really enjoy finding faster/better/cheaper ways to do something.</u> We have a specific way that we've always done this. Can you tell me why we do it this way? Are you open to me looking for a faster/better/cheaper way?"

- If your boss pushes you for a different timeline, you can say, "<u>Based on my experience, this will take X days/weeks/months,</u> but I'm open to looking at it again. Can you tell me why we need it faster?"

- If your boss asks for frequent updates, you can ask, "<u>I think I'll have a meaningful update on this in X hours/days/weeks,</u> but I want to understand your expectations for updates and how you use them. Can you tell me your expectations for updates and whom you update?"

You might get some resistance at first, but eventually, your boss will learn to expect your questions and may adjust his communication.

TRUST

Micromanagement fundamentally is a trust issue. The victim feels untrusted, the micromanager does not trust his staff member's skills, time estimates, knowledge, or communication. One way to mitigate this trust problem is to build trust before you need it. If your team knows that you trust them and you've consistently demonstrated trust them prior to this incident, you *might* be excused one or two rare instances of micromanagement. But remember, trust is like a piggy bank. You make small deposits every day, but one big withdraw can break the bank.

WHY WE DON'T TRUST

Mistrust can be caused by a misalignment between a teammate's **perceived level of competence** and the micromanager's perception of a teammate's competence. Some teammates *think* they are experts, but the micromanager *thinks* they are novices. The micromanager treats them like a novice (frequent follow-ups, specific direction), but the teammates expect to be treated as an expert. There are two possible causes of this:

1. Dunning-Kruger Effect: This research shows that people of low ability rank their ability higher than it actually is

2. The leader has a poor understanding of a teammate's actual ability.

You need to **understand** *which of these is causing this misalignment* before you can address the situation.

Also, **be aware of any unconscious biases which might cause you to rate a teammate's competence lower or higher than reality**. Here are a few common biases:

- <u>Halo effect</u> – "This teammate is not; therefore, this teammate is incompetent."

- <u>In Group Bias</u> – "I have an MBA and this teammate has an MBA; therefore, this teammate is competent."

- <u>Confirmation Bias</u> – "I believe that this teammate is not competent; therefore, his failures tend to come to my attention."

- <u>Fundamental Attribution Error</u> – "This teammate's project failed. The teammate caused the failure" or "This teammate's project was successful. This teammate caused the success." This ignores the fact that a success/unsuccessful project is the result of many different factors rather than one teammate.

CHAPTER 19: HEARTS & MINDS

"The science of life is changing hearts and minds." – Gary Bauer

For nearly twenty years, my kids have asked me about my job. "Dad, what do you do?" For the last dozen years, I've been in people leadership and I tell my kids that I win hearts and minds. Let me explain.

Let's imagine that you manage a grocery store. You have a display at the front of the store that needs to be refilled regularly. If this display is full, you sell more products, which means more money. If the display is empty, you sell fewer products, which means less money. You have cashiers at the front of the store who can see the display. They would be the first to know that the display is out. How could you get them to fill the display?

Let me give you two options:

Option 1:

> Get all the cashiers together. Tell them they are responsible for keeping the display full. Set up the rules for filling the display. Monitor the display. If it's not full, remind them of their responsibility. Maybe set up a punishment or a reward for a full display. Monitor that. Etc...

Option 2:

> Get the cashiers together. Tell them about the problem. "Hey guys, I need some help. The display at the front of the store keeps emptying out – which is great! Customers love this product. I want to make sure we keep it full so they can keep buying it. Do you have any ideas about how to do that?"

You're going to hear some not-so-helpful ideas, but eventually, someone is going to say something close to your idea. Maybe like, "The cashiers can see the display. We could monitor it."

You immediately jump on their suggestion. "That's a great idea! Talk more about that." Ask questions that direct the conversation, like "Nice! So the cashiers notice the empty display. Then what?" Eventually, you end up with the same plan, the cashier's monitor the display and fill it. Heck, you could end up with a better plan. Who knows?

Regardless, you praise the plan and the person or people who came up with it. You thank them.

Which option will get done when you are on vacation?

In all likelihood, the second you are out the door, no one will fill the display given Option 1. But because it was their idea, there's a good chance that Option 2 will continue.

I consider my job as getting you to believe what I believe. I call that "changing hearts and minds". If I can get the cashiers to believe that filling the display is important, they will do it without me nagging them or monitoring them. They will do it because it is important to do it. I might need to thank them for doing it and praise them for doing it, but I won't need to monitor and nag.

If you have an educational background, you might see that Option 2 is derived from the Socratic method of teaching.

Here's the downside. You give up all the credit for ideas. As a leader, you might know what needs to be done. You might tell people what needs to be done. But to change their hearts and minds, they need to think it is their idea. They get all of the credit.

When people say what a great job your team is doing, you will point out your ideas that you helped them uncover.

That's changing hearts and minds.

CHAPTER 20: HIRING THE BEST

"We hire people who want to make the best things in the world." –
Steve Jobs

The secret of management is surrounding yourself with great people. You have great people and management becomes a lot easier. I have a reputation for hiring and keeping the best people and turning them into a great team. Here are my secrets.

Ideally, you have some good people on your team with potential already and you can develop them. However, if you are interviewing, how do you tell if someone is awesome? I'll tell you the story about interviewing Harry (his real name, used with his permission), an awesome systems administrator that I hired.

A little background. This was quite a few years ago. I remember this specific interview because of Harry's response and because of Harry's level of performance. I was interviewing for a systems administrator. I had a full staff but I was looking to upgrade a position. I had one specific guy in mind. He was okay but didn't show any potential (or desire) to improve. I had invested six weeks and hundreds of dollars in a training program to get him up to speed but it wasn't happening.

Harry was a recent college graduate. He had done some IT work in college but nothing out of college. He was working full-time at a decent factory job. The interview went pretty good. Harry seemed solid, wasn't going to break anything, showed some potential, was passionate about technology, and capable of learning our systems.

Harry and I had been talking for 45 minutes or so and I was closing out the interview.

> *Me: Listen, man. I'm going to tell HR to call you tomorrow and make you an offer and I'd suggest that you not take it.*

Harry: Why?

Me: You have a good full-time job. This is a temporary position. And if you come in here and aren't awesome, I will fire you day one. So you will be leaving something that is a known quantity, for something that is high risk for a boss with incredibly high standards. Let me be 100% clear. I'm not looking for "very good"; I have "very good". "Very good" is not good enough. I need "great". If you are not great, I will fire you. So tomorrow, you'll get the offer, just turn it down.

Harry: Well, they always tell you not to blow your own horn in an interview but... (looong pause)... I'm awesome.

Me: Cool man. Let's rock and roll.

Harry was right. He was awesome (and still is).

IDENTIFYING AWESOME TALENT

(1) **Define your standards during the interview process.** *I'm not looking for "very good". I need "great". I am a boss with incredibly high standards.* Insert your own standards here.

(2) **Define the consequences of not meeting those standards during the interview process.** *If you are not great, I will fire you. You are leaving a good job where you are successful for a risky proposition.* It's important to understand your standards and understand exactly what your company will allow you to do. If you say that you fire bad employees, you better have the capacity to execute.

(3) **Allow candidates to eliminate themselves.** Most people who are not up to your standards will not have enough faith in their ability to put themselves in a high-risk position*. This assumes that there is a risk. If someone is desperate for a job, they are looking for any job. This is another reason that I like contract agencies.

(4) **Enforce your standards.** If you are all talk (about high standards and consequences) during the interview, you might as well not bother. Actually, at that point, you need to reassess some things about yourself as a person and a leader.

CHAPTER 21: DELEGATING

"I trust the people who are working with me. I delegate." – Mario Draghi

Some leaders have a problem with delegating. There are a variety of reasons that someone might not want to delegate a task. Perhaps the manager is the best at doing it, perhaps it needs to be done quickly, or perhaps the manager doesn't want to cede a responsibility.

I ran into this at a very large multisite company. I was talking to another leader. This leader was very, very technically competent and was complaining about having to handle some technical tasks because no one on his team was as competent as he was.

I said, "When I started in IT, I was working the help desk, but desperately wanted to build servers. I asked the server guys if I could help them in my spare time and they gave me a project to handle on my own. I guarantee I did it totally wrong and they had to redo it completely. But then they gave me another project... and another... and another... Eventually, I knew what the hell I was doing. But I guarantee, for the first year, they redid everything I did. When you were starting out did you have any experience like that?"

He agreed.

I continued, "It would have been *easier* to do it themselves. It would have been *faster*. But if they hadn't given me the chance to fail, I would have never learned. Are you going to give your team a chance to learn?"

When you refuse to delegate something, you fail to develop your people. Even stuff that you <u>hate</u> to do might be something that someone on your team would love a chance to try.

For example, I had to write a monthly status report. I hated that damned thing. 20-pages every month and no one read it. We emailed it to 3,600 people on a distribution list because my boss felt like it justified his existence. I put a tracking beacon on it for several months to see who opened it. Two people. Me and my boss. That's it. I hate doing things that don't add value and I didn't want to inflict that useless waste of time activity on one of my staff. But it wasn't a waste of time to them. To one of my supervisors, it was an opportunity to be in charge of something that would prepare him for the next promotion. Cha-ching! Win-win!

DECIDING WHAT TO DELEGATE

Delegate everything you can. I call that "aggressive delegation". Delegate everything you <u>can</u>. Can is the keyword. Things you can't delegate:

- Anything that is illegal, immoral, unethical, or a violation of policy. For example, a professional engineer cannot delegate signing engineering designs. If the corporate policy requires that a manager approve expenses, you can't delegate that.
- That's it. Everything else is up for delegation.

Delegation does not cede your responsibility as a leader. For example, I once worked for a manager who didn't want to make strategic decisions. He dumped the strategic plan for his department on my lap. I put together a strategic plan for him and when his boss questioned him about the plan, he said, "I don't know. David made that plan. I didn't really like it."

Firstly, that's absolute cowardice and I lost all respect for that manager, but more importantly, delegating doesn't cede responsibility.

CHAPTER 22: HOW TO INTERVIEW

"When you start to prioritize hiring likable people within your organization, these likable people will attract other likable people." – Karen Salmansohn

The training offered to managers on interviewing is lackluster. Typically, HR sits you down and gives you a list of questions that you can't legally ask. At some very progressive companies, you *might* get training on their interview philosophy du jour (behavioral, technical, group, etc...) and any resources (blind skills/personality testing) that is available. Here's the problem that I've run into: all of those types of interviews have <u>answers</u>.

Any interviewing candidate worth their salt will Google your company, look on Glassdoor to read the interview questions that other interview candidates have faced, and read how to answer them. Take the standard opener: "Tell me about yourself." Google has 6.7 million results for the search "Tell me about yourself interview question". There are literal formulas on how to answer: what to say, what not to say, how much personal information to include, how much humor, etc...

How about, "tell me about your greatest weakness?" 1.69 million results.

"Do you prefer to work alone or in a team?" Everyone knows how to answer that question. You make some non-committal statement about being flexible, being able to work alone or work with a team, and you like both. Only a moron would say, "I hate working on a team" or "I can't work alone." This question has an answer.

What are you going to learn that isn't a recitation of some article that the interviewee read?

I like to ask interview questions that don't have answers.

Three (Types of) Questions That Don't Have (Right) Answers

First, make both choices valid.

Instead of asking "Do you prefer to work alone or on a team," I say "Sometimes I work best alone and sometimes I work best in a team. When do you like to work with a team and when do you like to work alone?"

By opening with the statement, I've acknowledged that both answers are OK, I just want to know <u>when</u> they work best in these situations. This forces them to be more honest. If they say, "I like to work in a group when it's an important project" that says one thing about them. If they say, "I like to work alone when it's an important project" that says something entirely different. You just need to listen and figure out what they mean.

Another question I ask: "Some people learn best by reading, some by watching a youtube or video, some in a classroom, some by one-on-one instruction, and some by working with their hands. We all learn differently. How do you learn best?"

Again, I've made all the choices valid. I've given the candidate permission to answer honestly. What I'm listening for: "do they know themselves?", "do they know how they learn?", and "does how they learn match how we plan on training them in the role?" If a candidate doesn't know how they learn best, *they may not be learners*. I like people that pursue self-improvement opportunities. Those people can tell me how they learn best because they've done it. I also want to make sure that their learning methodology aligns with my organization philosophy. If my company doesn't send people to classes, but they learn best in classes, they might be a bad fit. If I'm super busy and can't do one-on-one time, but they learn best with one-on-one time, they might be a bad fit.

170

Second, a Consistent Story.

"Everyone is necessarily the hero of his own life story." - John Barth

Instead of "tell me about yourself," I open with "tell me how this job is the next rung on your career ladder. Tell me how your experiences, jobs, and education lead you here, and how this job fits into your overall career trajectory."

I want a story showing a consistent path, leading to the job opening I have. I do a lot of things with this question: I acknowledge that I'm interested in their long term career, I recognize that I might not be the end of the road for this candidate, and I know they are more than this job. I also get to hear a story. If the story shows a consistent arc leading to this job, it makes me comfortable that the candidate will be happy in this job. If the story jumps around a lot without a consistent theme, I know the candidate doesn't have a defined career direction. If the story shows a consistent arc, but my opening doesn't fit in that arc, I can ask other follow-up questions.

For example, I was on a team interviewing for a staff-level human resources person at a $100M manufacturer. The candidate had a consistent career arc rapidly progressing to an HR director at a billion-dollar company. So, I asked, "why the big step backward?"

She said, "I want to get away from the pressure of leadership."

I said, "You've progressed really rapidly through your career. You don't do that without a lot of personal drive and ambition. I read you as more of a type-A person than a type-B person. Am I right?"

"Yes. I'm definitely type-A."

"How long is a type-A person going to be happy in a small manufacturer in a staff HR position, know that she could run it? Maybe run it better than the current HR director?"

"I don't know."

She turned down the offer.

Third, Where's Your Heart?

Someone once told me, "you can't motivate the unmotivated." Someone else told me, "everyone is motivated, maybe just not by work." I worked with a technician once who was all about bowling. He would leave work at 5 PM and hit the bowling alley five nights a week. He had a "Popeye Thumb." His bowling thumb was enormous with muscles from so much bowling that it looked like Popeye's forearms.

He wouldn't work a minute past 5 PM. He was very motivated... to bowl. Once I figured that out, it was a magic button. "Hey man, if you could get that project done ahead of schedule, I'll get you sponsored in that next semi-pro event you are in."

When I'm interviewing people, I want to know, where's their heart? Bowling? Family? Work? Money? Recognition? Learning? Titles? Friends? Time off? Competition? Progression? Opportunity? Contribution? There's not one question that will reveal this. You need to listen, and to watch.

For example, I was on an interview board meeting with an engineer. He monotonously intoned his impressive career achievements, his incredible scholastic accomplishments, and his career aspirations. I asked, "what's the last thing you lead outside of work?" His eyes lit up. He sat up in his seat, "I was co-captain of our college soccer team." He animatedly chattered about the fun he had and how he had led the team. When he stopped, I said, "when you were talking about work, you were slumped over in your chair and talking down at the table; when you talked about soccer, you lit up like a Christmas tree. Why aren't you excited about your job?" The 5-minutes that followed were more revealing than the entire hour before.

Another example, I once interviewed a candidate who would need to relocate away from his family, including his ex-wife and son. I knew he could do the job, but I wouldn't have his heart. His heart was (rightly) with his son. I said, "man, you shouldn't leave your family. It will break your heart." Thank God, he didn't take the job.

The Formula

The formula is that there is no formula. I can't give you a list of questions to ask, or someone will create a list of answers. Here's the idea: know what you want, ask open-ended questions to find out if the interviewees align with what you want, and listen (really listen with your ears and eyes) to the answers.

CHAPTER 23: HIRING FOR CHARACTER

"Somebody once said that in looking for people to hire, you look for three qualities: integrity, intelligence, and energy. And if you don't have the first, the other two will kill you." - Warren Buffett

Hiring the right person is one of the most critical functions a leader does. A great hire can change the energy, environment, and execution of a team. A poor hire can cause grief, loss of productivity, litigation, and possibly the leader's job.

When hiring, I advocate for attitude over aptitude. Most interview questions focus on answering the question: "Can you do the job?" But research has shown alignment with the cultural values of the organization is as important as the technical skills for employee performance. Good cultural alignment results in greater job satisfaction, identifying more with their company, better retention, greater commitment, and superior job performance.

So, is culture just a checkbox on the list? "Does he fit our culture?"

No, culture is not one item. As discussed, culture is the accepted system of attitudes, aptitudes, actions, and abilities that represents your organization's beliefs, values, and norms. These attitudes, aptitudes, actions, and abilities vary from organization to organization. Each of these attitudes, aptitudes, actions, and abilities have different weights and each of the weights varies from organization to organization.

How do you measure something as nebulous as a corporate culture? I recommend using a weighted scorecard. A weighted scorecard is a matrix assigning different weights to different attributes to create an overall numeric measurement of cultural fit.

For example, let's say your organizations' culture encourages honesty, teamwork, energy, and listening skills. These are all fine attributes. To create a weighted scorecard using these attitudes, aptitudes, actions, and abilities, design a table with one row for each of the attributes.

Cultural Attributes				
Honesty				
Teamwork				
Energy				
Listening Skills				

For each attribute, assign a weight. The weight should reflect the relative importance of each attribute. It may be tempting to give each the same weight but avoid this. Using the same weight will reduce the value of your scorecard. To ensure that each weight is unique, I recommend counting down from 10. For example, if I felt honesty was the most important attribute, energy was second, listening skills were third, and energy was last, my scorecard would now look like this:

Cultural Attributes	Weight			
Honesty	10			
Teamwork	9			
Energy	7			
Listening Skills	8			

For each applicant, give them a score from 0 to 4. Why start at 0? If an applicant does not demonstrate a specific cultural attribute, they get a 0. A score of 1 means the candidate demonstrated the attribute very weakly. A 2 means the candidate demonstrated the attribute weakly. A 3 means the candidate demonstrated the attribute strongly. A 4 indicates the candidate demonstrated the attribute very strongly.

Some people want a middle of the road option. 1-5 with 3 meaning "average"; however, by eliminating the "average" option, you are forced to have an opinion. It's easier to give a candidate an "average" score when you don't feel strongly one way or another. Eliminating that option requires you to take a stand.

For each candidate score each attribute and multiple the 0-4 rating by the weight. Add the individual weight scores to produce a final score.

	A	B	C	D	E	F
1	Cultural Attributes	Weight	Candidate 1	Weighted Score	Candidate 2	Weighted Score
2	Honesty	10		=$B2*C2		=$B2*E2
3	Teamwork	9		=$B3*C3		=$B3*E3
4	Energy	7		=$B4*C4		=$B4*E4
5	Listening Skills	8		=$B5*C5		=$B5*E5
6			Final Score	=SUM(D2:D5)		=SUM(F2:F5)

Consider two candidates. Candidate 1 is very honest and has great listening skills. She demonstrates good teamwork but is a little weak in displaying energy. Candidate 2 demonstrates great teamwork and energy. He seems pretty honest but is a little weak in listening skills. Tough call, right? Each candidate has two areas that are very strong, one that is strong, and one a little weak. No real red flags. How do you make a decision? Gut feel? Their handshake? Who do they know?

With a weighted scorecard, now you can examine the candidates with a little more objectivity:

Cultural Attributes	Weight	Candidate 1	Weighted Score	Candidate 2	Weighted Score
Honesty	10	4	40	3	30
Teamwork	9	3	27	4	36
Energy	7	2	14	4	28
Listening Skills	8	4	32	2	16
		Final Score	113		110

Candidate 1 scored 113 points. Candidate 2 scored 110 points. You have an answer.

The weights in this example are not set in stone. You need to determine the weight for your culture and needs but determine the weights prior to the interview (just to keep yourself honest). It's also helpful to one interviewer to establish the weights and another interviewer (who does not know the weights) score the candidate.

Personally, Warren Buffet's quote echoes in my mind during interviews and I always give honesty a very high weight. If I can't trust someone, everything else goes out the window.

CHAPTER 24: PUTTING A BOW ON IT

"Every new beginning comes from some other beginning's end." –
Seneca

You've made it to the end! The end of the book, but the beginning of a lifelong continuous improvement, systems-thinking approach to leadership. Congratulations!

Together, we've looked at the state of leadership (both good and bad), the systems that support this leadership, a non-prescriptive method of personal assessment, and how to evolve your leadership to become something amazing.

It's not going to be easy. The system wants to shove you back down into mediocrity. But I believe in you. I believe that you can become a great leader. I believe that you can make a difference in people's life.

Thank you for reading my book. If you have any comments or questions, you can reach me using the email in the About The Author at the end of the book.

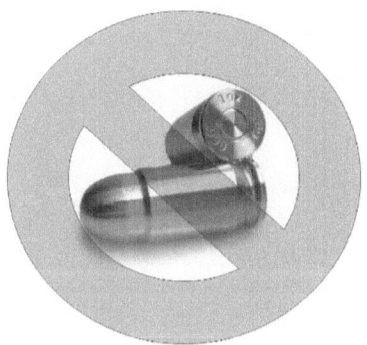

No silver bullets.

APPENDIX: THE UNFUCK LEADERSHIP © FRAMEWORK

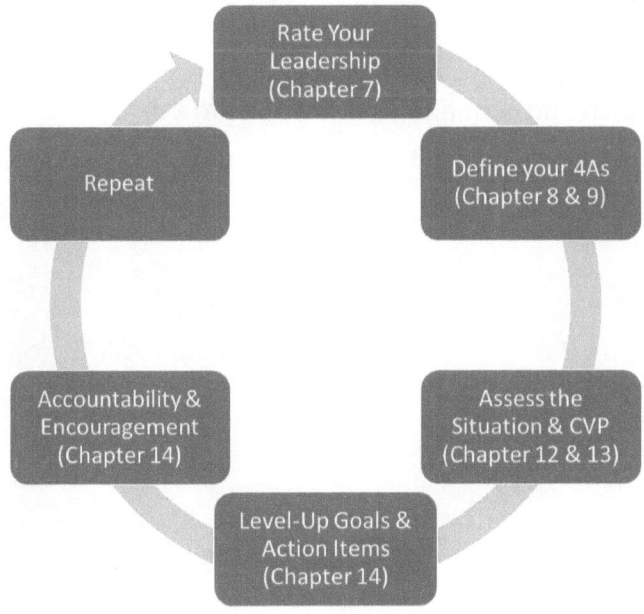

RATE YOUR LEADERSHIP — CHAPTER 7
Using Dunning-Kruger and my productivity scale establish a baseline score for your personal leadership effectiveness.

DEFINE YOUR 4AS — CHAPTER 8 & 9
Self-assess your aptitudes, abilities, actions, and abilities.

ASSESS THE SITUATION & CUSTOMER VALUE PROPOSITION — CHAPTER 12 & 13
Using the 4Ts, understand the environment in which you are and how your organization produces value (CVP).

SET PERSONAL LEVEL-UP GOALS & NEXT ACTION ITEMS — CHAPTER 14
Define your personal leadership growth goals and feasible, useful, connected, and keepable goals.

FIND AN ACCOUNTABILITY & ENCOURAGEMENT PARTNER – CHAPTER 14
Find someone committed to supporting you in the midst of your leadership growth plan.

REPEAT
Revisit your plan and continue your lifelong growth.

UNF*CK LEADERSHIP!

Character Sheet

Name: _____

Role: _____

Leadership Level (D-K Score): _____

Feedback Modifier (-10 to +10): _____

Aptitudes   Abilities

(1) _____   (1) _____

(2) _____   (2) _____

(3) _____   (3) _____

(4) _____   (4) _____

(5) _____   (5) _____

Other abilities _____

_____

_____

ABOUT THE AUTHOR

David G. Rettig has been married for 28-years to the only woman in the entire world with the patience to put up with his shit. He has three kids that think he's a great dad because they really don't know any better. There's a cat in his house who catches and eats houseflies. She may be a Flerken so he puts up with her. He loves weird people and weird things. He always tells his kids that everyone is weird, some people just hide it better than others.

David is the Chief Executive Manager of Synoptus, LLC, which provides Salesforce architecture and implementation services, business competency mapping, IT turn-around/cost reduction initiatives, and CIO advisory services.

David has a Bachelor of Science in Information Technology and M.B.A. from Franklin University in Columbus, Ohio, and a Master of Science in Management & Leadership from Western Governors University - Indiana. He's currently researching effective practices in leadership development as part of a Doctorate in business administration at Wilmington University, Wilmington, Delaware.

When not compulsively attempting to become a better leader, David serves as the membership chair for his local Mensa group, contributes to the International Society of Philosophical Enquiry, and plays board games. His current obsession is Gizmos. Great game.

If you would like him to speak or consult with your organization on unfucking your leaders, you can reach him at **david@unfuckitconsulting.com.**

www.ingramcontent.com/pod-product-compliance
Lightning Source LLC
Chambersburg PA
CBHW030629220526
45463CB00004B/1464